Buyer's Handbook for the Single-Family Home

Buyer's Handbook for the Single-Family Home

Steven James Lee, Esq.

VNR **VAN NOSTRAND REINHOLD COMPANY**
NEW YORK   CINCINNATI   ATLANTA   DALLAS   SAN FRANCISCO
LONDON   TORONTO   MELBOURNE

Van Nostrand Reinhold Company Regional Offices:
New York Cincinnati Atlanta Dallas San Francisco

Van Nostrand Reinhold Company International Offices:
London Toronto Melbourne

Library of Congress Catalog Card Number: 78-10206
ISBN: 0-442-23291-8
       0-442-23292-6 pbk.

Manufactured in the United States of America

Published by Van Nostrand Reinhold Company
135 West 50th Street, New York, N.Y. 10020

Published simultaneously in Canada by Van Nostrand Reinhold Ltd.

15 14 13 12 11 10 9 8 7 6 5 4 3 2 1

Library of Congress Cataloging in Publication Data

Lee, Steven James.
  Buyer's handbook for the single-family home.

  Includes index.
  1. House buying—United States. I. Title.
HD1379.L34   643   78-10206
ISBN 0-442-23291-8
ISBN 0-442-23292-6 pbk.

This book is dedicated to
my son, Justin Steven Lee.
It is hoped that he will
remember that nothing in
the world takes the place
of persistence and
determination.

ACKNOWLEDGEMENTS

The author wishes to express his thanks to the people who made this book possible:
Alberta Gordon—for her managerial efficiency amongst chaos.
Patricia Mansfield—for her sharpened red pencil.
Jim Ruth—for his amazing talent to produce many thoughts in a single drawing.
Karen Athena Lee—for taking over my baby-feeding shifts so I could write.

PREFACE

Dozens of volumes on the subject of real estate have been written for legal scholars and professional speculators. However, many of the intricate problems covered in these works are of little use to the layperson seeking basic information on buying a house. *Buyer's Handbook for the Single-Family Home* distills that large body of knowledge into its most essential components and presents them in straightforward language for the average home buyer.

To increase your ability to make a wise purchase, read the entire text before attempting the calculations contained in the worksheets. Once you have done so, tear out the worksheets, and use them as you go through the process of locating and buying a house. If you do this with reasonable care and attention, there is an excellent chance that the house you buy will provide you with both physical comfort and financial security.

STEVEN J. LEE, Esq.

Contents

1. Deciding to Buy

THE SINGLE-FAMILY HOUSE

For most people, the great American dream is to own their own home. Buying a house is often the single largest purchase and investment in a lifetime. Unfortunately, the average person buying a house is not adequately prepared to judge the quality of the purchase. In the early stages, the buyer usually neglects to analyze the rent-versus-buy decision, which inevitably leads to unnecessary financial strain and sometimes to loss of the entire investment. The second most common oversight occurs when the buyer views the house as a complete unit instead of as a collection of independent systems. A house is really a network of systems that fulfill human desires and needs. For example, there is a shelter system, a heating system, water and waste system, electrical system, and various work systems, such as a kitchen, which enable people to perform specific activities.

Thus, the potential buyer of a house with an expensive plumbing (or other) system should be prepared to inspect it thoroughly. All too often, however, the same buyers who would devote weeks to reviewing data on comparable automobiles will barely look at an equally expensive plumbing system. Their excuse is that since they know little about plumbing, they cannot judge its condition. Nothing could be further from the truth. Even a child can observe poor water pressure, sinks that don't drain, rusty pipes, and toilets that don't stop running.

From 1970 through 1976, the median income in the United States rose 47%. In that same period, the cost of maintaining an existing house jumped an estimated 73.4%, and the cost of maintaining a new house went up a whopping 102.3%. A buyer's failure to intelligently inspect a potential new home may well add large repair costs to already high maintenance expenditures.

In 1950, the typical new home had approximately 895 square feet of living space. By 1976, this living area had almost doubled so that the typical new house now has approximately 1590 square feet. Along with growth in size has come an expansion of amenities. In 1977, two-thirds of the new houses built in the United States had two or more bathrooms, most had large modern kitchens, and many had two-car garages.

Land is a major component in the price of a home. The cost of land currently

accounts for almost 25% of building costs, and this is reflected in a higher purchase price in many areas. There is a real scarcity of desirable residential property around urban employment centers. In addition, restrictive zoning practices such as 1-acre minimum lot sizes and ecological regulations have had a great impact on the remaining unimproved land. Such regulations make it more expensive to develop new homes.

Building materials have also surged dramatically in price. In the last 10 years, the cost of lumber has gone up 400% and the cost of cement has risen 60% in the last 5 years alone. Since it's unlikely that prices of materials will be reduced, it is to the buyers' advantage to know that what they purchase will not have to be repaired or replaced in the near future.

Between 1970 and 1976, the median price of existing housing in the United States rose 65% to $38,100, and the median price of new housing rose 89% to $44,200. It has been estimated that the typical new American home will cost about $78,000 in 1981. And that estimate is by no means for a luxury home. It is for the standard size and common amenities desired by the typical buyer.

When you consider buying a house, remember that homeownership involves many daily responsibilities. All of the systems in a home require fine tuning on a regular basis. In addition, lawn mowing, snow shoveling, painting, and a thousand other odd jobs will require some of your time. Even if you are not particularly handy, it is likely that the cost of hiring professionals will inspire you to learn basic carpentry, painting, and plumbing.

OTHER HOUSING ALTERNATIVES

There are other kinds of housing that may be more suitable to your budget or your life-style. A cooperative is a multiple-unit property in which buyers purchase shares of stock and receive a long-term lease to occupy a specific unit. A condominium affords an owner a recordable deed to a specific unit in a multiple-unit property, together with an undivided interest in the areas and facilities that are shared with co-owners. In both of these, the normal upkeep expenses are shared by all of the owners.

Cooperative and condominium developments have the advantage of facilities such as swimming pools, tennis courts, and clubhouses with the cost being spread out over numerous owners. On the whole, they can deliver more of these luxuries than the average homeowner can afford to provide. In addition, much of the maintenance is performed by employees instead of by an individual owner. The main disadvantage noted by condominium and cooperative buyers is a lack of privacy and complete control. The unit owner agrees at the time of purchase to go along with the decision of the majority. Sometimes, this means the owner must help pay for facilities or services that are not totally desired.

In recent years, many types of prefabricated houses have been developed. Such homes are partially assembled in a factory and then shipped to a building site for erection. Because labor is one of the largest costs in housing construction, handy individuals may be able to save thousands of dollars by performing the labor themselves or with the aid of family and friends. However, this book is not designed to consider the purchase of prefabricated shelter. Such a decision requires special knowledge of building codes, site preparation, and quality of materials, which are too detailed for the average home buyer.

Mobile homes are another alternative to the conventional single-family house. Today, more than 5 million Americans live in mobile homes in special parks or, where zoning permits, on their own property. Although such homes are relatively small, they offer the attraction of mobility. There are particular problems regarding quality of materials and design of a mobile home that do not apply to the conventional home. In addition, mobile homes tend to depreciate rather than appreciate; built-in equipment is generally not of the highest quality; mortgage financing seldom exceeds 10 years and involves higher interest rates; and inspection must rely more on the opinion of experts, such as structural engineers. Still, many of the principles for purchasing a conventional home, which are covered in the following chapters, can be adapted to analyze mobile-home purchases.

Even with these alternative types of shelter, for many people the great American dream is still a home of their own. How well they can enjoy that dream will depend in large measure on how much care they put into their decision to purchase.

RENTING VERSUS BUYING

The first aspect to consider in deciding whether to buy is how prudent it is to enter into a long-term mortgage commitment. Owning a home ties up a large down payment and diverts a substantial amount of one's monthly cash flow from other investments such as stocks, bonds, and savings accounts. For most people, buying a home means a change in life-style in order to accommodate mortgage payments. In addition, real estate is not easy to dispose of on short notice. In fact, homeowners often have to wait for a certain season of the year or for an improvement in the availability of financing to sell their home at its maximum value.

Single-family houses, when financed through conventional sources, normally require a down payment of 15% to 30% of the purchase price, However, government programs and certain builders can sometimes reduce the down payment to a very small amount or even to no amount at all. The average interest charge on a mortgage is 9%, but this varies throughout the country from 8% to 10½%. Twenty years ago, it was common for a seller to help the buyer complete the purchase by extending a purchase-money mortgage on favorable terms. Today, such transactions are rare since most sellers need the entire proceeds at sale in order to secure another home.

Buyers often overlook the advantage of forced savings produced by a mortgage. In terms of investment, buyers should consider whether they save regularly for future expenses and whether these savings are invested attractively. A mort-

gage forces the buildup of equity over a long period of time. In the first 10 years or so, most of the monthly mortgage payment is applied toward paying interest. As time goes on, more and more of the money is used to repay the principal amount borrowed. Each dollar of borrowed money that is repaid is forced savings, invested in homeownership. Table 1.1 gives some idea of how forced savings accumulate as the balance of the principal amount is repaid over time.

You can get some basic ideas about the cost of renting shelter versus the cost of owning shelter by making the computations on Worksheet 1. There is a common rule of thumb that suggests that buyers should spend no more than 30% of their income for housing nor purchase a home with a market price greater than approximately 2½ times their total annual gross income. Of course, if buyers can reasonably expect their earning power to increase in the near future, strict application of such rules may not be suitable. It is sometimes best for buyers to consider rising income and to extend this rule of thumb into larger and more attractive shelter that they believe they can afford and will want in the future.

Tax benefits are available to the property owner who files an itemized return. Homeowners can deduct the interest they pay, real-estate taxes, and school taxes, and in some areas can receive homestead tax exemptions. In many places, these benefits are available on the state and local level as well as on the federal tax return. Such tax benefits lower the cost of owning a home by providing an indirect government subsidy, a privilege that renters do not enjoy.

Although there are many subjective elements to homeownership, most of them

Table 1.1 Percentage of Mortgage Loan Remaining

Interest Rate	Loan Remaining After					
	5 years	10 years	15 years	20 years	25 years	30 years
Life of mortgage—30 years						
7%	94%	86%	74%	57%	33%	0%
7½	95	87	75	59	34	0
8	95	88	77	60	36	0
9	96	89	79	63	39	0
10	97	91	82	66	41	0
Life of mortgage—25 years						
7%	91%	79%	61%	36%	0%	
7½	92	80	62	37	0	
8	92	81	64	38	0	
9	93	83	66	40	0	
10	94	85	69	43	0	
Life of mortgage—20 years						
7%	86%	67%	39%	0%		
7½	87	68	40	0		
8	87	69	41	0		
9	89	71	43	0		
10	90	73	45	0		

boil down to control. Free of lease restrictions, buyers can have any size family in a home, keep pets, remodel according to taste, and more completely control the quality of life. However, a property owner is making a significant investment of capital, which a renter does not have to do. Thus, a buyer must have excess income above the satisfaction of day-to-day needs to service mortgage payments on the property.

After you have read this book and understand the information contained herein, you may wish to use Worksheet 1 to work through a series of hypothetical purchase prices (e.g., 2, 2½, and 3 times your annual income). Your mortgage lender can tell you about terms of financing such as the required down payment, duration of the mortgage, monthly mortgage payments of principal and interest, approximate legal costs, and settlement costs. Appendix III will allow you to calculate the amount of monthly installment payments on a mortgage with a term of 15 to 30 years at various interest rates. Remember that this payment will include both principal repayment and interest costs. Settlement costs needed to make the comparison on Worksheet 1 will be explained in detail in Chapter 7. Maintenance may be estimated as 1% of the purchase price per year, and does not include any major repairs required after purchase.

PERSONAL PREFERENCES AND NEEDS

Inflation has had a dramatic impact on the purchasers of private houses. Today, 6 out of 10 first-time buyers are composed of families where both the husband and wife are employed. This means that buying a house often requires the financial commitment of both spouses and a redirection of family spending patterns.

There are no hard and fast rules that enable buyers to decide what kind of house is most suitable. When the purchase involves an entire family, it is helpful to have a family discussion and then to consider each member's preferences. Of course, these will have to be balanced with the needs and financial resources of the family as a whole.

If buyers look at their family's preferences and needs, it will be apparent that some factors will change over time. Therefore, they should consider the age of family members, stability of employment of each member, likelihood of additional persons coming into the family unit, possibility of moving from one location to another, and the impact of mortgage-payment responsibility on other competing interests (e.g., vacations, education, cars, entertainment).

Beyond these factors are some highly subjective decisions. Buyers of single-family houses should consider whether they like to maintain a home and if they wish to become part of a community. They should also investigate the many types of shelter available to see what style would be best for their needs. Thousands of design variations exist for single-family houses. Some of the more common styles are:

WORKSHEET 1
RENT OR BUY?

1. Basic Information on House

Purchase price $_____

Closing costs $_____

Amount of mortgage $_____

Interest rate on mortgage   _____%

Amount of living space   _____ sq ft

2. Cash Invested in Shelter

Rent		Own	
Deposit on lease	$_____	Down payment	$_____
Moving expense	_____	Moving expense	_____
Necessary repairs	_____	Necessary repairs	_____
		Settlement costs	_____
Initial cash invested	$_____	**Initial cash invested**	$_____

3. Monthly Cash Outlay

Rent		Own	
Rent	$_____	Fire insurance	$_____
Apartment dweller insurance	_____	Homeowners insurance	_____
Pass-through expenses[a]	_____	Mortgage interest payment[b]	_____
		Mortgage principal payment[b]	_____
		Total taxes	_____
		Heat	_____
		Electricity	_____
Total monthly cash outlay	$_____	**Total monthly cash outlay**	$_____

4. Overall Comparison

	Rent	Own
Initial cash invested	$_____	$_____
Initial cash invested × Gross income	$_____	$_____
Total monthly cash outlay	$_____	$_____
Monthly cash outlay as % of monthly income	_____%	_____%
Total living space	___ sq ft	___ sq ft
Cost per square foot per month	$_____	$_____
Yearly mortgage-interest deduction	None	$_____
Taxes and other yearly deductions	None	$_____
Mortgage forced savings after:[c]		
5 years	None	$_____
10 years	None	$_____
15 years	None	$_____
20 years	None	$_____
25 years	None	$_____
30 years	None	$_____

5. Future Market Value of House

Purchase price	$_____
Appreciation rate per year	_____%
Estimated future market value in:	
5 years	$_____
10 years	$_____
15 years	$_____
20 years	$_____

[a]In some cities, landlords may pass on certain rising costs such as heating and real-estate taxes to tenants who have signed leases that bind them to pay such additional expenses.

[b]To compute the combined interest and principal monthly mortgage cost, refer to Appendix III. Assume that 10% of the payment is for mortgage principal and 90% for mortgage interest.

[c]Table 1.1 indicates the balance of the mortgage loan still outstanding after each five-year interval.

Tudor. A Tudor is usually an older house, has two- or three-stories, and is characterized by large wooden beams on the exterior and interior. Most older Tudor homes have large ornate fireplaces, small casement windows, slate roofs, and stucco exteriors.

Colonial. A colonial is a multistory home that usually has a large center hall with a staircase. Most are of wood construction, and some have large pillars at the outside entrance.

Ranch. A ranch house is ideal for buyers who dislike stairs since all rooms are on one level. It requires more land than multiple-story structures, and construction cost is higher because of the larger foundation, heating system, and roof. Currently, this is one of the most popular housing styles.

Victorian. A favorite style 50 years ago, a Victorian house is characterized by ornate woodwork inside and out, along with a wraparound porch outside. Often, there are three or four stories and front and rear staircases to the second floor. Many Victorian homes have stained glass windows and balconies.

Split-level. Split-level homes are divided, with less than a full story between levels. Usually, living quarters and household-activity areas are separated. A more modern style, it is ideal for construction on uneven building lots.

Mediterranean. Popular in warmer climates, the Mediterranean house often has an exterior of light-colored materials, which reflect heat. The roof is made of round, clay tiles, which drain well. Metal ornamentation is common on windows and doors.

Cape Cod. Constructed around a large, central chimney, a Cape Cod house generally does not have a full second story. It has a pitched roof designed to prevent the buildup of snow.

Because it is usually difficult and expensive to add space on to an existing structure, the buyer may be wise to anticipate future needs by purchasing more shelter than presently needed. Although this will increase the amount spent, it could prove an intelligent decision in the long run when one considers moving costs, settlement costs (see Chapter 7), and relocation of family members.

Table 1.2

	Advantages	Disadvantages
Old House	1. Generally higher quality construction. 2. Landscaping is completed. 3. Built-ins and carpeting may be included in sale. 4. Neighborhood is well-established. 5. Buyer often gets quick increase in value if house can be modernized.	1. Often needs major update of plumbing, electrical, or heating system. 2. May require a larger amount of cash to buy. 3. Appliances are often old and need replacement.
New House	1. Buyer can customize to own taste. 2. Financing is generally for greater percentage of price. 3. Has modern conveniences.	1. Often has higher taxes to offset new sewers, schools, etc. 2. Generally needs new lawn and shrubs or trees. 3. If in a development neighborhood, it is hard to judge who will move into unsold homes.

Another major consideration is whether to buy an old house or a new one. As shown in Table 1.2, there are definite advantages and disadvantages to both decisions.

FUTURE MARKET VALUE

It is not unrealistic for buyers to calculate the future market value of a house because they will sell it some years after purchase. Such an estimate in not a certainty of profit but rather a yardstick of expected return on an investment. To calculate the future market value, you must first choose a rate of appreciation per year. Statistics have indicated that between 1970 and 1976, the median price of existing housing rose at a compounded rate of approximately 9% per year and that of new housing rose almost 11% per year. However, these rates would probably be too high for reliable results starting from today's market. The runaway rise in prices of houses between 1970 and 1976 is likely to moderate in the future.

A more conservative approach is to choose an appreciation rate per year between 2% and 5%. Your estimate of the rate should be based on a feel for local market conditions, stability of the neighborhood, previous increases in selling prices, and the condition and size of the house in relation to surrounding homes. Most licensed brokers have a good idea of what to expect in yearly appreciation, and you can poll several to get a consensus of opinion. Local real-estate boards, attorneys who specialize in real estate, and bankers are other sources for this advice. In any case, be realistic in making your estimate. For example, a $50,000 home might appreciate as shown in Table 1.3.

Table 1.3

Appreciation per Year (%)	Future Market Value After			
	5 years	10 years	15 years	20 years
0	$50,000	$50,000	$50,000	$50,000
1	52,551	55,231	58,048	61,620
2	55,204	60,950	67,293	74,297
3	57,964	67,196	77,898	90,306
4	60,833	74,012	90,047	109,556
5	63,814	81,445	103,946	132,665

VACATION HOMES

Although most houses are purchased as a principal place of residence, there is a growing demand for vacation homes. In fact, a recent survey estimated that some 2 million Americans now own a second home. Many urban dwellers who rent their shelter wish to participate in the equity buildup and tax advantages of real estate. In addition, some buyers do not wish to search for accommodations during the crowded tourist season. For people who vacation in the same place each year, a suitable home may well cost far less than expensive rented facilities.

There are numerous housing developments in recreational areas that are designed to be second homes. Most are built intentionally smaller and without unnecessary conveniences such as multiple bathrooms, separate dining rooms, enclosed garages, and, in some warmer climates, expensive heating systems. In general, the purchaser of a vacation home gains access to some kind of recreation facility such as a beach, hunting area, or ski slope.

Some apartment dwellers purchase small farms in rural areas as a kind of retreat from city life. Unfortunately, there is a higher possibility of robbery and vandalism when a home is infrequently occupied. Another potential problem with such a minifarm is the absence of playmates for children. One positive element, however, is that often a local farmer will sharecrop the excess land and provide income that may be used to offset expenses.

Buying a vacation home with one or more partners can be risky. There are always the problems of scheduling occupancy periods and assigning responsibility for repairs. Moreover, homes are not extremely liquid investments. Thus, they cannot be converted into cash as easily as, for instance, stocks or bonds. If a problem develops in one partner's finances, the other(s) may be forced to provide the total funds for upkeep.

If you already own a home that is your principal place of residence, you should review the tax laws before purchasing a vacation home. Second homes afford only limited tax advantages unless they are used by the owner for a brief period of time each year.

In selecting a vacation home, buyers should apply the same standards used for any single-family house. Checking out good materials and construction, community facilities, proper financing, resale value, taxes, access to highways, electrical service, drinking water, and the many other points presented in this book will insure the value of your investment.

HOW TO DEAL WITH THAT DOWN PAYMENT

What if you have decided that homeownership is for you, and your monthly cash flow seems to permit such an investment? However, the initial down-payment requirements seem to be beyond your financial abilities. Here are some tips to help you accumulate the necessary cash or dispense with a down payment altogether.

The Federal Housing Administration insures mortgage loans made by conventional lenders. These insured loans often permit the buyer to obtain better terms and lower down payments than would otherwise be available. If the house is not yet built, the FHA allows a down payment of only 3% of the first $25,000 of FHA-appraised value and 5% thereafter, up to a $60,000 guarantee limit. If the house has been constructed within the preceding year, but without an FHA appraisal, it is still possible to apply for an FHA-insured mortgage. In such a case, the FHA insures the house at a percentage of its appraised value. This will require a larger down payment—about 10%—but still less than the 15% to 30% that conventional lenders require without FHA guarantees.

As a general rule, the FHA allows a 30-year repayment term on the mortgage. Most conventional mortgages, on the other hand, are written for a period of 20 or 25 years. The longer term permits lower monthly mortgage payments for buyers with cash-flow problems. Interest rates on FHA-guaranteed mortgages are usually less, and prepayment provisions are less restrictive.

If the buyer or the buyer's spouse is a veteran, then the Veterans Administration can assist them in buying a home. The VA will guarantee the mortgage loan for 60% of the purchase price or $17,500, whichever is less. Lenders find a VA mortgage a better credit risk because they know that they will recover at least $17,500 if the buyer fails to repay the mortgage. In rural areas where there is a scarcity of conventional lenders, the VA will lend money directly, up to a maximum of $17,500.

Saving is, of course, the primary means most people use to amass the down payment on a home. Under normal circumstances, you should automatically save 10% or more of your total monthly income. However, once you have decided to purchase a private house, it is not unusual to discipline yourself or your family to save 50% of your monthly income for one or more years. Of course, this will mean doing without many of the other things that compete for your income.

Okay, what if you have located the castle of your dreams at a great price but you don't have enough saved to cover the down payment and settlement costs? The first thing you might do is liquidate any long-term assets such as savings bonds or stocks. If this is still not sufficient, consider selling some of your

personal property such as an unnecessary car, stereo equipment, an expensive camera, or a coin or stamp collection.

The second resource is to borrow money either against an expected tax refund, anticipated bonus, or inheritance. Also check your life insurance policy to determine if it has built up enough cash-value equity to cover the down-payment shortfall. Finally, ask your parents or relatives for a low-cost or interest-free loan. Don't be embarrassed. Chances are that they did the same thing when they first purchased a home.

If you do borrow part of the down payment, work out a method to pay it back on terms you can live with. Be realistic, and allow for unforeseen but almost inevitable expenses, such as emergency medical bills or unexpected repairs. However, make it a point to pay back these funds as quickly as you can. This will leave you with the peace of mind that you home is properly financed with your own equity.

WHAT IS THE FIRST STEP?

The first step in buying a home is to determine where you will enjoy living. The proper neighborhood will add to your satisfaction as well as increase the value of your investment. Take some weekend drives through the areas that appeal to you. Then get down to business, and assemble the following information:

Local history. Usually obtainable from chamber of commerce or town hall.

Local map. This should indicate local points of interest. You can also use this map to locate the proximity of individual homes to shopping, schools, factories, and fire department.

Zoning regulations. Find out how the residential neighborhoods are protected. The changeover of residential land near your home to commercial use can harm the value of your investment.

Population and income levels. Available from the United States Bureau of the Census. Many libraries also have this information.

Taxes. Speak to the local tax authority, and get rates for school and property taxes for the last five years.

Market prices of shelter. Many local real-estate boards or associations of brokers can furnish the market prices of shelter. If they cannot help, speak to a title insurance company.

Doing this kind of homework can be dull and time-consuming. However, considering the magnitude of the investment you are contemplating, it is time well spent. Armed with the preceding information, you will be able to deal more intelligently with real-estate brokers, make more accurate appraisals of neighborhoods, and generally feel more secure with the house you purchase.

2. Searching for a House

USING THE NEWSPAPERS

An ideal source of information about the opportunities available in single-family houses is the local newspaper. If you properly analyze the real-estate advertisements, you will determine what types of houses are available and what prices prevail in a particular area. Most local papers have a classified real-estate section, which lists offerings under "Houses" or "Single-Family Houses." It is a good idea to find out which local newspaper has the most extensive real-estate coverage. (Often, it is the paper that publishes a large, multisection, Sunday edition.)

NEWSPAPERS ARE
AN IDEAL SOURCE
OF INFORMATION
ON HOUSING!

After you start to review real-estate listings, you will become familiar with the advertising terminology. This shorthand enables advertisers to communicate details about a property in a minimum of advertising space. Some of the most common abbreviations follow:

A/C	air-conditioned	**lndry**	laundry
ac.	acre	**LR**	living room
applnc	appliances	**md's**	maid's room
bal	balcony	**mint**	excellent condition
bch	beach	**mod**	modern
blt	built-in	**mstr**	master bedroom
BR	bedroom	**mtg**	mortgage
brk	brick	**nr**	near
bsnt	basement	**occup**	occupancy
bth	bath	**pnld**	paneled
burg/fire	burglar and fire alarm	**pfl of**	professional office
C/H	center hall	**pvt**	private
cent air	central air conditioning	**rm**	room
con	convenient to	**schls**	schools
ctr	center	**scpd**	landscaped
dbl	double	**sep ent**	separate entrance
dk	dining room	**shwr**	shower
DR	deck	**sld dr**	sliding doors
EIK	eat-in kitchen	**spklr**	underground sprinkler
fam rm	family room	**starter**	smaller first home
fin	finished	**steam**	steam heating
flr	floor	**terr**	terrace
fml	formal	**txs**	taxes
fpl	fireplace	**w/**	with
gar	garage	**W/W cpt**	wall-to-wall carpet
gas	gas heating	**wbf**	wood-burning fireplace
ht air	hot-air heating	**xtr**	extras
ingrnd	in-ground pool	**yd**	yard
in-law	separate apartment	**yng**	young
lib	library	**yr**	year
lge	large		

To build a basic awareness, review, on a daily basis, the real-estate listings for areas that interest you. Form a library of the Sunday real-estate sections so you can refer to them at a later date. It's a good idea to learn the names of brokers who advertise regularly. From their offerings, you can determine which firms specialize in certain communities or types of houses.

Beware of communities or neighborhoods that have a relatively large number of homes for sale. This could be a barometer of the falling desirability of the area to potential home buyers. Rapid turnover usually results in a decrease in the underlying value of real estate.

Become familiar with the various types of financing packages available in the areas of interest. These are generally offered by the developers of new homes. If a small down payment is important in your search for a private home, pay particular attention. In many cases, the down payment and mortgage terms are made very attractive to induce buyers to choose a new home instead of an existing one. Don't hesitate to make telephone calls to inquire about the details of such developer financing. This research will give you an excellent picture of the comparative cost of borrowing.

If you find a home that interests you, refer back to your collected newspapers and compare the asking price to the prices of comparable housing in the area. A price that is too low should make you more cautious during your inspection of the house and property. A higher price should be justified by some added value not in the surrounding houses such as a pool, central air conditioning, large grounds, or expensive interior improvements. Even so, avoid paying the highest price on the block if you possibly can.

When you are purchasing a house, it is sometimes possible to buy directly from the owner, thus avoiding a brokerage fee. Since the normal brokerage fee is several thousand dollars and is usually paid by the seller, some portion of the savings will probably be given to the buyer through a reduced purchase price. If you want to attempt to buy directly from a seller, look for ads that say "owner." The principal drawback of doing this is that the selection of houses will be greatly reduced. In fact, in most desirable areas, it is uncommon for an owner to undertake the effort and incur the expense of a direct sale.

Proper use of newspaper real-estate information means you must be able to quickly screen potential homes without wasting time on detailed investigation. Toward that end, *avoid* the following:

- Houses priced well beyond your finances.
- Homes that lack an element your family desires such as an eat-in kitchen or a fireplace. Of course, you can add amenities once you purchase, but generally this is an expensive proposition.
- Houses that have extras you do not want and probably can't afford, such as swimming pools, excessive land, or additional bedrooms.
- Unbelievably low prices. You can be sure that such ads are come-ons.
- Homes outside the areas you have selected. It is far better to concentrate your search than to be hopping all over the place.
- A house that has very high taxes compared with those of comparable homes in the area. This will make it difficult to resell the house at a future date.

USING YOUR FEET

Never underestimate the value of plain old footwork. The best bargains in private homes rarely show up in newspaper ads. They don't have to because they are snapped up by aggressive buyers. This section offers some of the techniques used by such buyers.

Local banks sometimes have to foreclose and sell a home when the buyer is unable to meet the mortgage obligation. In many cases, the bank is only interested in recovering its mortgage funds, and thus a qualified buyer can get a bargain purchase. Speak to the mortgage officer at your local bank, and determine the possibility of being considered when and if a foreclosure occurs. Of course, the drawbacks here are a lack of selection and uncertainty of success.

It is becoming more common for a prospective buyer to place an ad in the real-estate section of the newspaper. This small investment may pay off very handsomely, because a prospective seller is likely to review the listings of comparable homes before contacting a broker. If he or she sees your ad, it might lead to direct contact. Since such ads are expensive, they should contain enough information to allow the seller to qualify on location and price level. Sometimes, further details such as number of bedrooms or style of home can be listed.

Word of mouth may put you in contact with a potential seller at a very early stage. So, if you know people who live in an area that interests you, let them know you would consider buying a home nearby. However, don't leave your friends completely on their own. Tell them your price range, style of home, number of bedrooms, and other important details. It may even be helpful to give them a copy of Worksheet 2, which contains a detailed description for brokers.

USING A BROKER'S SERVICES

A licensed real-estate broker earns a commission fee based on a percentage of the sale price that a buyer pays for property which the broker has shown. Broker commissions vary, but generally they range from 5% to 7% of the sales price. In most cases, the seller pays the brokerage fee, and that reduces the net proceeds received from the sale.

A broker is a trained real-estate salesperson, not a mind reader. Therefore, before you telephone a single broker, write up a detailed description of your housing needs and desires and those of your family. The more specific the description, the less time you will spend viewing unsuitable homes and the less chance you will have of buying the wrong one. Some things to consider before you write the description are:

- What style house do you prefer?
- How many bedrooms do you need?
- Do you plan to have (more) children?
- Is a family room or den important?
- How many bathrooms are necessary?
- Is a shower or a bathtub preferred?
- Do you want an eat-in kitchen?
- Do you want a fireplace?
- Is a rural setting or a development more appealing?
- Do you prefer an old and quaint house, or a modern one?

- What communities interest you?
- How much money do you want to spend?
- When can you move into a new home?
- How much land do you need?
- What are the highest taxes you can afford?
- Do you need a garage? What size?
- Can you afford to remodel? To what extent?
- Do you prefer corner property?
- Would you live on a busy street?

Gather the preceding information on Worksheet 2, and from it type up a brief description to give to brokers. Good brokers act as a clearing center for marketable private homes. When they have a specific description of what you're looking for, they will perform a screening process, which can save you many a wild-goose chase.

When you are out looking at houses with a broker, don't trust what you see to memory. Take along a notebook, and in it keep a record of:

1. Owner's name
2. Location
3. Asking price
4. All local taxes
5. Yearly heating costs
6. Yearly electricity costs
7. Number of bedrooms
8. Number of bathrooms
9. Special features
10. School district

This basic information will help you narrow down your choice. Next, you should perform the detailed inspection that will be discussed in Chapters 3 and 4.

A word of advice: remember, people usually work hardest for the party who pays them. Real-estate brokers work for a commission, which is based on the selling price and paid by the seller. Consider this before you rely on the oral advice of, or information supplied by, a broker. Thoroughly checking out the facts is ultimately the buyer's responsibility.

PURCHASE PRICE AND MONTHLY CASH FLOW

The marketplace of available single-family houses usually has a trade-off between monthly cash flow and purchase price. Monthly cash flow consists of the monthly burden of paying heating and electricity costs, real-estate taxes, school taxes, other taxes, insurance, and mortgage payments. As a rule, the higher the monthly cash-flow costs among comparable homes, the less desirable the property and thus the lower the purchase price. In terms of potential purchasers, there are usually more buyers who desire lower monthly cash-flow expenses.

A particular house's monthly cash flow is affected by many external factors. Heating bills and electrical rates vary widely among different areas of the country. Taxes are primarily a function of the demands for public services in a particular community. Even fire and homeowners insurance rates depend on the proximity of a house to fire and police departments. All of these factors will affect your purchase price as well as resale potential.

For example, let us compare Home A, a split-level with three bedrooms, two bathrooms, and monthly cash-flow costs of $950 per month, with Home B, a private house in a neighboring community. Home B, a similar split-level with three bedrooms and two bathrooms, on a similar plot of property, has monthly cash-flow costs of $1113. The purchase price for Home A is $84,000, and we can obtain mortgage financing for 25 years at 8½% for $63,000. The purchase price for Home B is $72,000, and we can obtain a 30-year, 8% mortgage for 90% of that amount.

We might question whether Home A is overpriced. Perhaps, but all other things being equal, more buyers are willing to put up a larger down payment on a

WORKSHEET 2
DESCRIPTION FOR BROKERS

Maximum purchase price $\$$_____

Maximum monthly carrying costs $\$$_____

Style preferred   _____

Number of bathrooms   _____

Number of bedrooms   _____

Occupancy date desired   _____

Positive Attractions (check and number in order of importance)

☐ Age of homeowners in area _____

☐ Close to schools   _____

☐ Commuting convenience   _____

☐ Corner property   _____

☐ Den   _____

☐ Eat-in kitchen   _____

☐ Family room   _____

☐ Fireplace   _____

☐ Gardens and grounds   _____

☐ Handyman's special   _____

☐ Landscaping   _____

☐ New house   _____

☐ Older house   _____

☐ Size of development   _____

☐ Size of village   _____

☐ Sunny exposures for plants _____

☐ Two-car garage   _____

Other Comments: _____

_____

_____

_____

_____

Request from Broker

Local street map
Local history
Listing of area banks
Statement of commission charges

Table 2.1. Cash-flow costs of Home A and Home B.

Monthly Expense	Home A	Home B
Heating	$ 84.00	$ 218.00
Electric	22.00	21.00
Real-estate taxes	145.22	166.37
School taxes	109.00	107.00
Other taxes	32.00	76.00
Fire insurance	20.00	22.00
Homeowners insurance	30.00	27.00
Mortgage payment	507.78	475.63
Total	$950.00	$1,113.00

higher purchase price if the monthly cash-flow costs will be lower. However, we should examine whether the monthly carrying costs are subject to change by the new owner. Sometimes, a small investment can dramatically change the expenses of operation.

The monthly cash-flow costs of Home A and Home B are presented in Table 2.1. Our breakdown of monthly cash flow shows that the heating costs of Home B are extremely high If we can correct the heating problem by installing $2000 worth of insulation, then it might be wise to consider Home B for our investment. Home B is priced $12,000 less than Home A and requires a down payment of only $7200 (.10 × $72,000), whereas Home A needs a down payment of $21,000 (.25 × $84,000). The lower down payment should leave us with enough funds to correct the insulation problem.

MONTHLY CASH FLOW AND NET MONTHLY COST

A correct analysis of the cost of owning and operating a single-family house must be computed on an *after-tax* basis. As stated, monthly cash flow is the amount paid each month for heating, electricity, real-estate taxes, school taxes, other taxes, insurance, and mortgage payments. *Net monthly cost* is what is actually paid per month during the year, after all available tax savings are subtracted from monthly cash flow. Therefore, we can divide our monthly cash-flow expenses into nondeductible items and tax-deductible items, as shown in Table 2.2. Once we have made this division, the net monthly cost can be calculated by computing

Table 2.2. Breakdown of cash-flow expenses.

Nondeductible	Tax-Deductible
Heating	Real-estate taxes
Electric	School taxes
Fire insurance	Village taxes
Homeowners insurance	Mortgage interest payments
Mortgage principal payments	

the tax savings in the tax-deductible items and subtracting the result from the monthly cash flow. Thus, we arrive at the formula:

Monthly Cash Flow	−	Tax Savings in Deductible Items	=	Net Monthly Cost

For simplicity's sake, assume that 90% of monthly mortgage payments will go toward interest charges. This number will work well enough to furnish a good idea of the net monthly cost. Use Appendix III for the calculation of the total monthly mortgage cost including interest. Then enter 90% of the computed figure on line 4 under "Add Tax-Deductible Items" on Worksheet 3.

CALCULATING NET MONTHLY COST

Using Worksheet 3, we can calculate the net monthly cost of any single-family house you might consider buying. Comparison of the results will give you an

Table 2.3. Expenses of Home A and Home B.

Expenses	Home A	Home B
Initial		
Closing costs	$ 2,000	$ 2,000
Down payment	21,000	7,200
Repairs	0	2,000
Mortgage balance	63,000	64,800
Monthly		
Heating	$ 84.00	$ 84.00
Electricity	22.00	21.00
Real-estate taxes	145.22	166.37
School taxes	109.00	107.00
Other taxes	32.00	76.00
Fire insurance	20.00	22.00
Homeowners insurance	30.00	27.00
Mortgage payment	507.78	475.63
Total	$950.00	$979.00

WORKSHEET 3
CALCULATING NET MONTHLY COST

Monthly Cash Flow

Add Nondeductible Items

    1. Heating $_____

    2. Electricity   _____

    3. Fire insurance   _____

    4. Homeowners insurance   _____

    5. Mortgage principal payments[a]   _____

A. Total Nondeductible Items $_____ $_____

Add Tax-Deductible Items

    1. Real-estate taxes $_____

    2. School taxes   _____

    3. Other taxes   _____

    4. Mortgage interest payments[a]   _____

B. Total Tax-Deductible Items $_____ $_____

Total Monthly Cash Flow (A + B) $_____

Tax Savings

Multiply

Total tax-deductible items × Individual tax bracket = $_____

Net Monthly Cost

Subtract

    1. Total monthly cash flow $_____

(minus) 2. Tax savings   − _____

Net Monthly Cost $_____

---

[a] Assume that 90% of the monthly mortgage payment calculated from Appendix II is interest expense and that the balance is principal repayment.

HOME A
CALCULATING NET MONTHLY COST

Monthly Cash Flow

Add Nondeductible items

1. Heating	$ 84.00	
2. Electricity	22.00	
3. Fire insurance	20.00	
4. Homeowners insurance	30.00	
5. Mortgage principal payments	50.78	
A. Total Nondeductible Items	$ 206.78	$ 206.78

Add Tax-Deductible Items

1. Real-estate taxes	$ 145.22	
2. School taxes	109.00	
3. Other taxes	32.00	
4. Mortgage interest payments[a]	457.00	
B. Total Tax-Deductible Items	$ 743.22	$ 743.22
Total Monthly Cash Flow (A + B)		$ 950.00

Tax Savings

Total tax-deductible items ($743.22)	$\times$	Individual tax bracket (.35)	=	$ 260.13	

Net Monthly Cost

Subtract

1. Total monthly cash flow	$ 950.00
(minus) 2. Tax savings	−260.13
Net Monthly Cost	$ 689.87

---

[a] Assume that 90% of the monthly mortgage payment calculated from Appendix II is interest expense and that the balance is principal repayment.

HOME B
CALCULATING NET MONTHLY COST

Monthly Cash Flow

Add Nondeductible Items

1. Heating	$ 84.00	
2. Electricity	21.00	
3. Fire insurance	24.00	
4. Homeowners insurance	27.00	
5. Mortgage principal payments	45.56	
A. Total Nondeductible Items	$ 201.56	$ 201.56

Add Tax-Deductible Items

1. Real-estate taxes	$ 166.37	
2. School taxes	107.00	
3. Other taxes	76.00	
4. Mortgage interest payments[a]	428.07	
B. Total Tax-Deductible Items	$ 777.44	$ 777.44
Total Monthly Cash Flow (A + B)		$ 979.00

Tax Savings

Total tax-deductible items ($777.44)	$\times$	Individual tax bracket (.35)	=	$272.10

Net Monthly Cost

Subtract

1. Total monthly cash flow	$979.00	
(minus) 2. Tax savings	−272.10	
Net Monthly Cost	$ 706.90	

---

[a] Assume that 90% of the monthly mortgage payment calculated from Appendix II is interest expense and that the balance is principal repayment.

excellent idea of the financial commitment involved in purchasing a specific property. You should weigh these results against your financial resources before making the final decision to purchase.

Let's carry out the calculations on Worksheet 3 for Home A and Home B. We will assume that Home B is insulated properly and thus has the same heating costs as Home A. In Table 2.3, expenses for Home A and Home B are listed. Home A has a $63,000 mortgage at 8½% for a 25-year term. From the mortgage tables in Appendix III, we can calculate that Home A has a total monthly payment (principal and interest) of $8.06 per thousand dollars or $507.78 (63 × $8.06). On Worksheet 3, we divide this monthly payment into 90% interest expense and 10% principal repayment.

Now we will calculate the effects of available deductions on the monthly cash flow. If the buyer's federal taxable income is in the 35% tax bracket, then on Worksheet 3, 35% of each of the ''Tax-Deductible Items'' will be saved at tax time. So, for Home A, there is a total tax savings of $260.13 (.35 × $743.22). This monthly tax savings is then subtracted from our total monthly cash flow to give us net monthly cost of $689.87 ($950.00−$260.13).

Home B can be purchased with a 30-year, 8% mortgage for $64,800. From Appendix III, we can calculate that the total monthly mortgage payment will be $475.63 (64.8 × $7.34). Once again, divide this amount into 90% interest expense and 10% principal repayment. We will also assume that the buyer is in the 35% tax bracket for federal income-tax purposes. We can then perform the calculations contained in Worksheet 3. (Remember, we have reduced heating costs by $134.00 per month by installing proper insulation.)

If we review the calculations for Home A and Home B, it becomes apparent why houses must always be compared on an after-tax basis. The monthly cash flow for Home A is $950 and for the properly insulated Home B $979, which is a difference of $29 per month. However, once tax advantages are calculated, the net monthly cost of Home A is $689.87 and of Home B $706.90, which is a difference of only $17.03. In Home A, tax savings reduced actual monthly cash outlay by $260.13 ($950.00−$689.87) and in Home B by $272.10 ($979.00−$706.90). Therefore, remember that tax savings significantly reduce the monthly cost of homeownership. They also affect the relative cost of operating one home versus another depending on how much of the monthly cash flow is comprised of tax-deductible items.

3. Exterior Inspection

THE LOT

Location and surface topography are important determinants of property value. For example, in the Rocky Mountains, land sells for $50 per acre, while in downtown Chicago, San Francisco, and other urban settings, it sells for as much as $1 million per square block. Rocky Mountain land is remote and undeveloped, whereas urban land is readily usable and conveniently located.

Land is one of the major costs in the construction of shelter, and it presently accounts for 25% of the purchase price of a house. Therefore, before you sign anything, get a good idea of the quality of the land under your prospective home. Check to see that the earth around the foundation is graded so that water will drain away from the house. In new housing projects, inquire about the subsoil, especially if the lot was filled in. It is essential that the fill used under the house be suitable for that purpose. Otherwise, the ground could settle and cause cracks in the foundation or even more extensive damage. Proper grading and quality fill help prevent erosion damage to landscaping as well as the house itself.

There are certain high-risk areas in the United States that are subject to floods, high tides, earthquakes, and mudslides. Not all of these risks are covered by insurance, and so a home buyer is flirting with tragedy. Even in established communities there are areas that are notorious for flooding during springtime. You should ask the broker and town inspector if such areas exist in the community. Remember, if it is not properly controlled, a small stream bordering a home can swell enormously during the spring.

Landscaping is an important feature of any home. Trees, hedges, stone walls, and flowering bushes are expensive if you have to buy them. In addition, they are necessary for aesthetic appeal, privacy from neighbors, and a degree of weather protection. Consider such items a valuable part of your total investment.

Many buyers prefer the corner lot on a quiet, residential street. It offers more light because the border on several streets separates it from other homes and also provides an added degree of privacy. Buyers can expect to pay slightly more for a corner-lot house because of these advantages. One rule of thumb is to allow for about 25% more on the price of the land sold with a corner house. Of course, this assumes that the size of the parcel and its overall character are similar to other lots in the neighborhood. If it is larger than other parcels or contains specific favorable characteristics, a corner lot can add a great deal of money to the purchase price.

ORIENTATION ON THE LAND

The land under a house should be large enough to allow for proper positioning. House orientation is important in terms of view, natural light, heating costs, and aesthetic appeal. For example, in northern climates, a house should maximize its southern exposure. Since the sun rises in the east and sets in the west, a southern exposure receives more sunlight than any other exposure. The sun will warm rooms with large windows and substantially reduce heating bills. In a southern climate, it is best to have a house face north to reduce air-conditioning costs.

In winter, in the United States, the sun rises in the southeast and sets in the southwest. By midsummer, the sun has changed to a high position whereby all areas enjoy sunshine. Careful buyers will also note the size and position of the shrubs and trees to see if they block much of the sun's heat. Ideally, shade trees should lose their leaves in the winter to allow the sunshine through.

DRIVEWAY AND GARAGE

The driveway to a house should be usable in all seasons of the year. However, steep grades or sharp turns may make it difficult to maneuver a car in winter months. Beware of driveways that descend steeply from the street into the garage. In a heavy rain, these can cause flooding as water cascades down the slope and into the house. The surface of the driveway is also important, both aesthetically and because it determines how difficult snow and ice removal will be in areas with harsh winters. Cement and paved surfaces such as macadam are generally more desirable than stones because they last longer, provide better traction, and give a more finished appearance to the property. Cracks or buckling in the driveway may indicate an improper subsurface preparation. Be alert for such problems.

The size and location of the garage are also worth noting during your inspection. Many homeowners use their garage for additional storage space. Also, a garage attached to the house is more convenient as it provides direct access into the home. If yours is a two-car family and you are considering a home with a one-car garage, remember that in colder climates, a car deteriorates more rapidly when it is left outside all winter.

PATIOS, DECKS, AND WALKS

In recent years, there has been a sharp increase in the number of private homes that have been constructed with or that later added on outdoor patios and decks.

These worthwhile improvements make the land more usable and valuable. Just be certain that they are correctly constructed to withstand the problems of climate in the area. In the North, patios and decks should be strong enough to prevent buckling from freezing and thawing. A deck located on a beach should be able to withstand any high tide or storm. Decks constructed in the sandy soil of the South should have foundations that will not slip. Of course, in all cases, there should be proper drainage away from the house.

On the whole, redwood is the most desirable wood for outdoor decks. It resists insects and weather better than most other common woods. Concrete is the most durable surface for walkways. However, it is not always the most aesthetically pleasing, and many homeowners prefer brick or flagstone because they are more colorful. On the other hand, weeds may grow between bricks or flagstones that are not embedded in cement. This requires regular upkeep, which is time-consuming.

ROOF

Although it is difficult to inspect the roof from the ground, certain obvious flaws can be detected. These include areas that are barren of roofing material, valleys or depressions in the surface, corroded flashing, and rotten gutters and downspouts. Also look for rust spots on the outside of the house; these indicate that there is improper drainage or a leak that will probably require immediate repair. Since a roof surface is not particularly expensive to replace, it is unwise to reject an otherwise basically sound property simply because the roof needs fixing. A better approach is to make allowances for the cost of replacement in your bid.

Figure 3.1 illustrates the five most common roof designs.

Fig. 3.1. Five most common roof styles.

The most popular roof coverings are:

Slate. Slate is the most expensive roofing material, but once installed it should last for the life of the house. Sometimes slates are damaged by falling branches or sliding ice. Replacement is difficult and should be done by a professional.

Wood shingles. Although wood shingles were very popular at one time, they have recently been restricted because they are a fire hazard.

Clay tile. Clay tile is used mostly in warmer climates. In cold areas, clay tile would crumble after continuous exposure to snow and ice.

Asphalt shingles. Asphalt shingles work well in almost any geographic area. Certain fire-safe, high-quality shingles can last up to 25 years, so inquire about the quality used.

Asphalt tar. Asphalt tar roofing material works well on flat roofs. A layer of roofing felt is covered with the tar, in which small gravel or marble chips are then embedded to reflect the sun's heat. It may last from 5 to 25 years, depending on the number of layers applied.

Roll roofing. Roll roofing is asphalt sheet material, which is rolled onto the roof surface and cemented. The least expensive roofing material, it is not recommended for flat surfaces.

Aluminum. Use of aluminum in roofs is relatively new. Although such a roof should have a long life, inquire about the specific product used in its construction and ask if it is guaranteed. A reputable roofing firm can give you an indication of the quality and durability of the specific materials.

EXTERIOR SURFACE

The outer walls of a house provide strength to the overall structure, protection from the elements, and insulation. Thus, a careful buyer will take the time to walk around a house and observe the quality and condition of its exterior. In a development where the house has not yet been constructed, the buyer may want to specify the quality of exterior materials that the contractor must use. There should always be a first covering of gypsum or lumber sheathing attached to the wood framing. This provides support as well as insulation. All outer coatings such as siding, masonry, or stucco should then be attached to this first covering.

One of the most common outer walls is clapboard siding, which consists of boards, 6 to 8 inches wide, with a tapered edge at the top. Clapboard is nailed on and then painted with several coats of quality paint. Kept properly painted, an exterior surface of clapboard should last indefinitely. Check to see that the boards are free of curling or twisting. (Boards that are not lying flat will have to be nailed in tightly or else replaced.) If the paint is full of blisters, you should figure the cost of a new paint job into your bid.

Masonry walls are another popular exterior. Although more expensive than clapboard, they require less maintenance. Masonry walls can be of brick or cut stone. Sometimes the bricks are glazed, which gives them the additional quality of masonry walls; large cracks usually indicate severe foundation settling. Before you buy a house with large cracks, have a professional engineer inspect it.

Cement stucco is a common exterior surface in many northern climates. It consists of a cement mixture put on top of metal lath, which is attached to the first covering. Very often, hairline cracks appear in stucco, but they are not cause for alarm since they are easily repaired. However, be alert for major cracks or large sections where the stucco is not firm and tight to the wall. On the whole, stucco is more expensive to replace than other outside surfaces.

Aluminum siding is an ideal exterior surface for any area. Most aluminum siding has built-in insulation, which reduces heating and air-conditioning costs. In addition, aluminum is virtually maintenance-free since it does not rust or require painting. In many cases, aluminum siding has been put on an older house because the exterior surface had become unsatisfactory. Inquire about the type of aluminum siding used, and satisfy yourself that it is of high quality and properly installed. Generally, it is not necessary to bring in a professional to assess quality and expected life of the siding. In many cases, the owner will know the product used, and a telephone call to a reputable installer will give necessary details.

DEVELOPMENT PROJECTS

If you are considering purchasing a house in a new development area, some inquiry is in order. Find out—from local banks, real-estate boards, or experienced brokers—if the builder's previous projects were successfully sold out. Determine whether certain improvements such as roads, curbs, sewer, recreational facilities, and power lines are the responsibility of the developer or of the surrounding community. If you discover that the builder has been unreliable in the past, it is best to shy away from the purchase.

Find out what the maximum size of the development will be. You may move into a small community only to find that it is expanding to hundreds or even thousands of homes.

If the designs of the houses are all similar, it can put a ceiling on the resale price. Many buyers prefer to live in areas where the homes are not alike because they enjoy variety. This usually is found where construction was done by different builders over a period of time.

One advantage of buying a home that has not yet been constructed is that you can contract for the use of specific materials. For example, you can pay for extra insulation, aluminum siding, high-quality windows, additional bathrooms, larger water heater, or lumber treated with chemicals to be fireproof. Adding such things during construction will increase the price modestly, whereas the same alterations in an existing home would be extremely costly and, in some cases, impossible.

EMPLOYMENT

The most overlooked factor in the purchase of shelter is the employment prospects in the area. Before you commit yourself to long-term mortgage payments, assess the scope of industry in the local community. Since buying a house is a decision to ''put down roots,'' be sure the area offers opportunities for attractive employment.

Settling in a ''company town'' where there is one major employer can endanger your entire investment if that employer's business turns sour. Not only might you be unemployed, but there may also be no buyers for your home. So, before buying in a company town, look into the size and stability of the main industry.

THE COMMUNITY

The desirability of a particular home reflects the quality of services in the surrounding community. A pattern of living will develop in an area because of the demands of its taxpayers. For example, a community with many young parents is likely to place considerable emphasis on building or maintaining educational facilities and playgrounds. Conversely, there are areas with large older popula-

tions favoring lower taxes because many residents have to live on fixed incomes. The educational programs in such areas may be poorly funded compared to surrounding communities.

Following is a partial checklist of important components of suburban living. If possible, locate these important services on a community map to get an overview of how a particular house is situated in relation to these services.

Fire Department
  Where is the nearest firehouse?
  Is there a fire-hydrant system? (This will affect fire insurance premiums.)
  Where is the nearest fire-alarm box?
  Has the fire department inspected the house recently?
Police Department
  Is the area adequately patrolled?
  Is there a history of crime in the area?
Food Stores
  Can you walk to food stores?
  Is there adequate competition?
General Shopping
  Is there a full-service business district nearby? Department stores?
Recreation
  Is there a safe playground nearby?
  Does the community support a swimming pool? Playing fields for organized
    sports?
Sanitation
  How efficient is garbage collection?
  Does the town cart the garbage away, or is a private firm employed?
Medical
  Is there a hospital nearby? With an emergency room?
  Does it have modern equipment?
Water and Power
  How do local electricity rates compare with surrounding areas?
  Is there a complete sewer system?
  Have there been problems with water supply in summer?
General
  Where is the nearest appropriate house of worship?
  Is there a theater or other entertainment nearby?

LOCATING COMMUNITY INFORMATION

Before "putting down roots," it is a good idea to get a clear profile of the community. There are numerous sources of statistical data, and it is up to you to decide how thorough you should be. Some sources of valuable information are:

- The *U.S. Bureau of the Census* is an excellent source for information on population, employment, housing, income levels, and numerous other facts.
- The *U.S. Department of Housing and Urban Development* publishes a free report on housing each month.
- The *county recorder* can provide information on building permits, zoning, and codes in the local area.
- The *local real-estate board* will often be aware of the trend of housing costs in the community.
- The *local tax assessor* is a basic source of information on taxes and their trends over the last five years.
- Local *newspaper files* are a good source for reliable information on risks in the area, such as flooding or mudslides.
- *Insurance companies* can supply the rates on homeowners insurance, and an agent can provide information about crime in the community.

EXHIBIT 3.1

Comparison Receipts and Disbursements for School Years 1974–75, 1975–76, 1976–77, with Budgets for 1977–78 and 1978–79

	ACTUAL INCOME AND EXPENSES			BUDGETED	
School Year: July 1–June 30	1974–75	1975–76	1976–77	1977–78	1978–79
BALANCE AND RECEIPTS					
Balance	$ 728,736	$ 861,552	$ 830,569	$ 741,626	$ 561,626
Taxes	4,232,830	4,566,247	4,933,833	5,307,661	5,577,067
State Aid	984,003	1,004,462	1,004,332	935,281	988,500
Other Receipts	243,209	150,638	152,247	75,268	86,500
TOTAL BALANCE & RECEIPTS	$ 6,188,778	$ 6,582,899	$ 6,920,981	$ 7,059,836	$ 7,213,693
Reserve for Encumbrances Previous Year	$ 111,623	$ 132,183	$ 124,910	$ 280,814	$ 192,508
TOTAL	$ 6,300,401	$ 6,715,082	$ 7,045,891	$ 7,340,650	$ 7,356,201
DISBURSEMENTS					
General Support	$ 759,588	$ 876,090	$ 863,094	$ 981,176	$ 1,001,729
Instruction	3,254,290	3,447,514	3,767,652	3,992,365	4,174,271
Pupil Transportation	68,016	68,820	80,344	94,265	102,670
Undistributed	1,224,772	1,367,179	1,423,987	1,580,404	1,623,397
TOTAL DISBURSEMENTS	$ 5,306,666	$ 5,759,603	$ 6,135,077	$ 6,648,210	$ 6,902,067
Reserve for Encumbrances	$ 132,183	$ 124,910	$ 169,188	$ 130,814	$ 154,134
Fund Balance—June 30	861,552	830,569	741,626	561,626	300,000
TOTAL	$ 6,300,401	$ 6,715,082	$ 7,045,891	$ 7,340,650	$ 7,356,201
Assessed Valuation	$63,771,153	$64,313,850	$65,235,250	$65,535,153	$65,605,663
Tax Rate per $1,000	66.3753	70.9995	75.6314	80.9895	85.0000
Enrollment	1,801	1,783	1,743	1,723	1,677
Per Pupil Cost	2,947	3,230	3,520	3,859	4,116
Per Pupil Cost—excl. Debt Service	2,703	2,975	3,299	3,615	3,928

SCHOOLS

One of the most basic services in any community is primary and secondary education. It is also the most expensive because of staffing and the need for modern facilities. In an area where the schools are crowded or the buildings are obviously old, you should be prepared for a large capital expenditure. Telephone the school board, and try to find out if plans are being readied for new community schools. If so, consider it a mixed blessing. On one hand, your taxes are likely to rise sharply, which may reduce property values. On the other hand, new schools attract homeowners who desire quality education for their children.

The quality of instruction can be fairly well judged by:

- Average class size
- Number of graduates who go on to college
- Types of colleges graduates attend
- Average score of senior class on standardized tests
- Quality of modern teaching aids, such as language laboratories
- Extracurricular activities available

A knowledgeable home buyer should be aware of what future school taxes in an area are likely to be. You should be able to obtain a copy of the annual report on the school budget. Calculate the average rate of increase over the previous five years, and compare it with budgets of surrounding communities. Exhibit 3.1 is an excerpt from such an annual report, prepared for a school district in New York State. Note that it shows the trend of costs over a five-year period to allow some anticipation of future increases. In the exhibit, the tax rate per $1000 rose 28% in five years, with an average rate increase of 7% per year.

4. Inspecting the Interior

If you are purchasing in an area where there are building codes, be certain that the builder has received a Certificate of Occupancy (see Exhibit 4.1). This indicates that an inspector has examined the house and found it in conformity with the building codes. (During the Closing of Title, you will receive a copy of the Certificate of Occupancy.) Nevertheless, building codes vary greatly in the kind of construction and materials they require. Thus, your own inspection will be your primary indicator of the quality of construction.

When you go to inspect the house, take along the following tools:

1. A 10-foot retractable tape measure with a stop button that can lock it in an open position
2. Clipboard or hard-backed pad for taking notes
3. Mechanical pencil
4. Red pencil
5. Graph paper on which you can draw a floor plan to scale
6. A ruler appropriate for making a scale drawing
7. A copy of Worksheet 4
8. Camera (optional)
9. Light meter (optional)

As you inspect the house, fill in the appropriate information on Worksheet 4. Pay close attention to the overall quality of construction in each area listed on the worksheet. Remember, it is unlikely that every feature will be perfect. Instead, look for superior materials, neatness in construction, and as many outstanding points as possible. The potential for creative adaptation of living space, such as converting an attic into a bedroom, is also important to consider.

When a particular home interests you enough to consider bidding on it, make up an overall floor plan. Measure the width and length of every room. An easy scale to work with is 0.5 inch equals 1 foot. Thus, if a bedroom is 13 feet long and

EXHIBIT 4.1

Certificate of Occupancy

BUILDING DEPARTMENT, TOWN OF NORTH JUSTINVILLE

MANHASSET, NEW YORK

Date .... March 10, 1937

37-91
A74565

This Certifies that THE BUILDING LOCATED IN Sec. No. .... 3 .... Block No. .... 46 .... Lot No. 89

Nassau County Tax Map, Address .... N/S Tallyrand Road, 108.21 W/Pickwick Road

Manhasset, New York

conforms substantially to the approved plans on file in this office, Permit No. .... 5176 .... Date .... Sept. 30, 1936

and to all requirements of the Building Zone Ordinance and Building Code of the Town of North Justinville, Nassau County, N.Y.

Zone .... Res A .... Occupancy .... One Family Dwelling and attached

One Car Garage

This certificate issued to .... Levitt & Sons

Owners

Address .... 135 Tallyrand Road, Manhasset, New York

Levitt & Sons

Owner—Builder—Architect

Address .... Manhasset, New York

.... Linda Capulli ....
Building Official

.... of the aforesaid building.

12 feet wide, you should draw a rectangle 6.5 inches long and 6 inches wide. (You may want to put each room on a separate page, and make up each floor later.) Locate windows on the floor plan, and mark in red pencil the location of electrical outlets. Be certain to note the location and size of hallways and stairways. (See Fig. 4.1.)

The purpose of an accurate floor plan is twofold. First, it allows you to calcu-

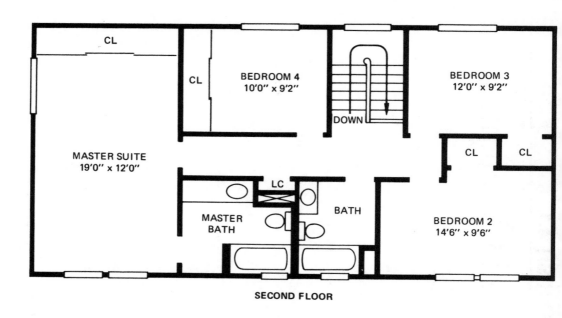

SECOND FLOOR

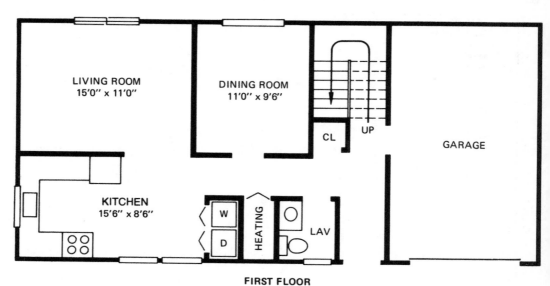

FIRST FLOOR

Fig. 4.1. Floor plan.

WORKSHEET 4
INSPECTION

Address _____ Date _____

_____

_____

Type of House _____

Exterior

Type of foundation _____

Type of exterior _____

    Condition _____

Storm windows _____

Screens _____

Type of driveway _____

Garage _____

Patio or decks _____

Roof

Type _____

Condition _____

Insulation _____

Ventilation openings _____

Exhaust fan _____

Interior

Walls

    Type _____

    Condition _____

    Paint[a] _____

    Insulation _____

Ceilings

    Condition _____

    Height _____

Type of heating _____

Plumbing _____

Fireplace _____

Placement of electrical outlets _____

Scale for Condition: E = excellent, G = good, F = fair, P = poor.

[a]Lead-based paint is hazardous to children.

Light level in rooms _____

Floors creaking _____

Closet space _____

Storage space _____

Air conditioning _____

Dehumidifier _____

Handrail on staircase _____

Windows

Type _____

Condition _____

Broken panes _____

Worn sash cords _____

Windowsills _____

Orientation of house (N,S,E,W) _____

Sufficient light for houseplants _____

Bathrooms

Condition of fixtures _____

Separate shower stall _____

Tile _____

Shutoff valves under fixtures _____

Medicine cabinets _____

Water pressure _____

Dripping faucets _____

Electrical outlets _____

Condition of bathtubs _____

Type of piping _____

Kitchen

Cabinets _____

Formica countertops _____

Range _____

  Type _____

  Model year _____

Oven _____

  Type _____

  Model year _____

Scale for Condition: E = excellent, G = good, F = fair, P = poor.

Dishwasher _____

    Type _____

    Model year _____

Refrigerator _____

    Type _____

    Model year _____

Disposal _____

Exhaust fan _____

Flooring _____

Lighting _____

Eat-in kitchen _____

Electricity

Number of amperes _____

Circuits in use _____

Breakers or fuses _____

Voltage _____

Miscellaneous

Size of garage _____

Recreation facilities _____

Lawns _____

Transportation _____

Shopping _____

Built-in features _____

Noise _____

Overall Comments: _____

_____

_____

_____

_____

_____

_____

_____

_____

_____

_____

_____

_____

Scale for Condition: E = excellent, G = good, F = fair, P = poor.

late the square footage of living space required on Worksheet 1. This in turn gives you the correct per-square-foot cost of shelter when you compare renting with buying. Second, you can use the scale drawing to plan how to fit your furniture into your new home. This should facilitate moving and perhaps save time and moving costs.

The following sections will discuss how to examine such important features of a house as the basement, framing, windows, walls, floors, and electrical, heating, and plumbing systems. Proper examination before buying should assure you of getting the best value for your money. So be careful in judging each of these items. Think of the expense of replacing each one as equal to buying a new luxury car.

BASEMENTS

A basement can be very functional if the space is not interrupted by numerous support columns. Even where such columns have been used in construction, they can generally be removed when alternate methods of support are installed. Check basement walls for major cracks and brownish stains. Hairline cracks are common and occur as the foundation settles. Larger open cracks, on the other hand, sometimes signal structural problems. Stains on walls or floors generally indicate

GIVE HIGH MARKS TO HOUSE,
WITH A FINISHED BASEMENT!

leaks or seepage from the outside. Waterproofing is relatively inexpensive, but you should get an estimate before you buy.

Give high marks to a house with a finished basement; the added area can serve as a family room, shop, or playroom. Also be alert to a house in which the basement has enough free space to be easily converted into a finished room. Such a job usually costs several thousand dollars but you are likely to get your money back should you sell the house.

In some areas of the country, houses are not constructed with a dug-out basement. Instead, they are either built on concrete slabs with reinforced steel rods or on footings. The poured concrete slab should be at least 4 inches thick and rest on a layer of gravel and sand. Footings are more difficult to judge, and a professional engineer should look at them for you.

The basic ingredients of our major inspection—such as heating plants, uncovered pipes, and exposed beams—are most visible in the basement. Where there is no basement, there is generally a crawl space that will reveal the same information. Be prepared to spend a considerable amount of time in these areas if you wish to do a thorough inspection.

FRAMING

The *framing* is the basic structure or "skeleton" of a house and supports its weight. If you are buying an existing house, there is little that can be done to change its composition. Perhaps weak areas can be supported or in some cases replaced. However, if you are purchasing in a development where the house is not yet built, obtain the specifics on framing construction. Here are some guidelines:

- *Floor joists* are located under each floor of a house. They should be made of at least 2-by-6-inch construction lumber. Sometimes, where there is a heavier load or a larger span, several lengths are nailed together. Many older houses have much larger, sturdier supports such as 6-by-8-inch timber beams.

  Floor joists should have wood bridging between them. This is done either in an X pattern or with solid wood. (See Fig. 4.2.)

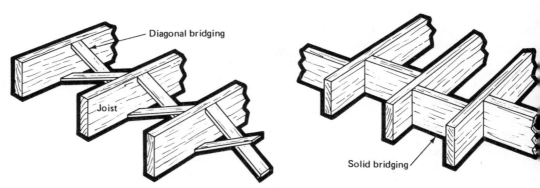

Fig. 4.2. Bridging of beams.

Houses are sometimes supported with wood over a steel beam. This kind of construction is usually found in newer homes.

- *Studs*. The basic wall and window frames are usually made from 2-by-4-inch construction-grade wood. On the outside, these are covered with plywood or gypsum board. On the inside, they are covered by wallboard, metal lath that is covered by plaster, or some other suitable material. Insulation is placed between the studs.
- *Roof beams*. Most roof framing is done with 2-by-6-inch construction-grade wood. In colder areas, the roof must support the weight of snow during winter, so strength is important. The roof beams should be braced in a manner similar to that of the floor joists.

Figure 4.3 shows typical framing to help you identify individual members.

Building codes in many areas specify the type and quality of materials to be used in home construction. They even specify how many inches there should be between wood supports. If there is a strict building code in the area and the home has been inspected by the building department, chances are everything is alright. But if you have doubts or if the building code is weak, call in an engineer.

WALLS

Walls are an important point to consider during an inspection. They not only serve as background for furniture, but they also provide insulation, noise barriers, and sometimes fire protection. Ask the seller about the general construction of ceilings and walls. In a cold climate, find out how well the walls are insulated.

There are two types of wall construction: *dry-wall,* which includes gypsum board, Sheetrock, paneling, and plastic-type covering; and *wet-wall,* which includes plaster, masonry, and brick. Wet-wall construction is substantially more expensive than dry-wall, because the walls take longer to complete and the price of materials is much higher. Wet-walls are usually sturdier and are better barriers to noise and fire.

Gypsum board or Sheetrock is the leading dry-wall material applied to interior walls. It is relatively inexpensive and comes in 4-by-8-foot panels, which cost about $4 each. Tape and compound are used to join the sheets to create a complete wall, which is then painted or wallpapered. Flame-resistant finishes are available in higher-quality Sheetrock. However, such details might only be available when the house is being sold prior to or during construction.

Kitchens should have proper wall covering. Water- and dirt-resistant vinyl wallpaper keeps a ditchen clean and new-looking for a long time. Also, it is a good idea to have tile or some other protection such as metal or glass on the wall behind a cooking range. Check for these features when inspecting a house.

Cracks in walls, common in older homes, usually occur because of the foundation settling. Small cracks are easy to repair when preparing a wall for painting. However, be cautious if whole sections of a painted wall are loose or flaky. This

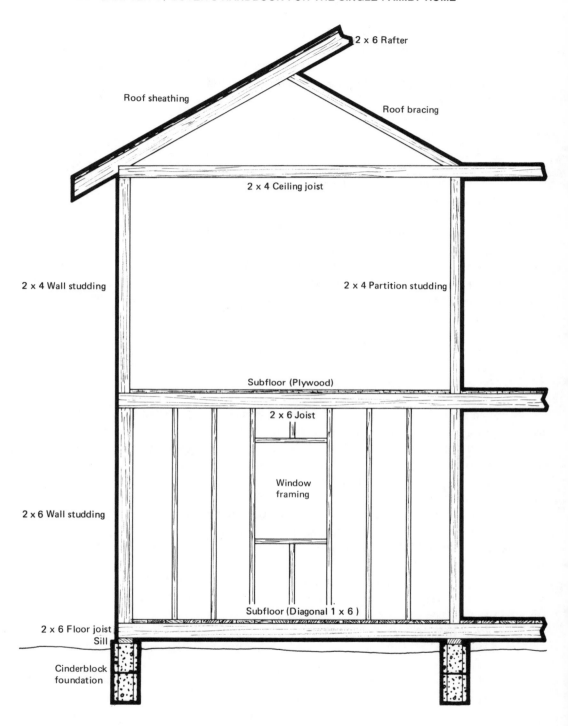

Fig. 4.3. Framing.

usually indicates that water is leaking from either the plumbing or the roof. Discolorations in the paint also indicate leaks, and you should feel such discolored areas with your palm to detect dampness. Also, check for lead-based paint, which can seriously injure children if they eat loose pieces.

If there's a fireplace, be sure that fireproof brick or stone has been used sufficiently. This means that there should be an area in front of the fireplace to catch any stray sparks that fly out when the fireplace is in use. Check for cracked bricks and loose cement. Finally, open and close the flue several times to be certain it works.

FLOORS

There are two principal kinds of finished flooring: hardwoods and synthetic materials. Both should be installed over adequate subflooring. The most common subfloor is ½-inch plywood, which is nailed to the wooden joists. Then the finished floor is added on top.

Hardwood floors are usually made from either oak or maple. Such wood is very expensive, and installation is time-consuming. Hardwood floors are common in older homes, but the expense has limited their use in most new construction. Today, when hardwood is used, it is installed for the most part in dining rooms, living rooms, and master bedrooms. Lower-grade flooring is used in other areas.

Hardwood for flooring is manufactured in several ways. The most widely used is a strip form that has a tongue and groove. Strips are fitted together and nailed in place. Also common is parquet flooring, which consists of small wooden tiles that are fitted and then glued to the subflooring surface. Check for squeaks in the wood flooring to determine how securely it was laid.

There are dozens of synthetic flooring materials. Most are vinyl-based and come in tiles or large sheets. A strong glue is used to anchor the flooring to the subfloor. Most synthetic flooring is extremely durable, which makes it ideal for high-traffic areas such as kitchens or entrance foyers. It also resists scuff marks and stains, and in damp areas it will not warp like wood.

DOORS

Doors provide security from intruders and also act as a barrier to noise or fire. In addition, doors are a good indicator of the quality of construction of a house. In the past, most doors were made from solid wood. In recent years, hollow-core doors have become popular with builders because they are substantially less expensive. Check to see that the main outside doors are made of solid wood, not with thin panels that could easily be pushed in. In all cases, open and close each door to be certain that it is properly set in the frame.

ELECTRICAL SYSTEM

The electrical wiring that travels through the walls and ceilings of a house is divided into circuits. Each circuit is protected by its own *fuse* or *circuit breaker*. There is generally a *panel box,* which centrally contains the fuses or circuit breakers. If too many appliances are on the same circuit or if bare electric wires are touching due to problems such as worn insulation, a fuse or circuit breaker will "blow." That is, the circuit will be interrupted, and electric current will not pass through the wires until either the problem is corrected or the circuit is reset. Without such safety devices, the hazard of an electrical fire exists.

When you inspect a home, always check the panel box. Older structures usually have fuse boxes (see Fig. 4.4). A fuse, which looks like a small, round glass bulb, screws into the panel box. On its top is a small window, which has a flat metal strip inside. When there is trouble in the electrical system, the fuse discolors and the metal strip melts. One disadvantage of a fuse box is that spare fuses must be kept handy in case one has to be replaced. Since fuses come in several sizes and shapes, this is something of an inconvenience. Also, fuse systems may not be able to handle heavy-duty appliances such as electric ranges, dryers, and air conditioners. In such a case, an expensive rewiring job might be required to improve the electrical system.

Circuit breakers are a more modern type of protection than fuses (see Fig. 4.5). When electrical trouble causes them to "blow," circuit breakers simply switch to the "off" position. Once the cause of the problem has been determined and

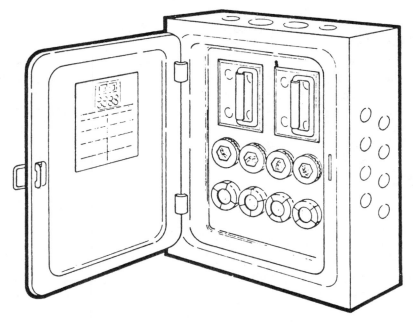

Fig. 4.4. Panel box and fuses.

Fig. 4.5. Circuit breakers and panel box.

corrected, a circuit breaker has only to be reset—by flipping the switch back to the "on" position. From the standpoint of convenience, circuit breakers are easy to use; unlike fuses, they do not have to be replaced. When inspecting a home, remember that circuit breakers also indicate a more up-to-date electrical system.

When examining the panel box, check to see that there are sufficient circuits for

convenient and safe use of electrical lighting and appliances. Each heavy-duty appliance should have its own separate circuit. Inadequate wiring does not mean that you must replace all wiring. In most instances, additional circuits can be added to the existing system. If you believe this to be the case, get a cost estimate from a licensed electrician before you buy.

While examining the panel box, check the amperage at which electricity is delivered. Just like the flow of water through a pipe, the flow of electricity is larger if it comes through a larger-diameter wire. Current is measured in amperes. Ideal service is from 100 to 200 amperes. If the house is equipped with an electric hot-water heater, electric range, electric washer and dryer, or several air conditioners, then 150-ampere service is the minimum acceptable current. Note too that three-wire service is better than two-wire, and it indicates that higher-quality materials were used in construction. You can identify the type of service by examining the electrical outlets. In three-wire service, each outlet has a round hole in addition to the two rectangular slits that accommodate the prongs of a plug.

Frequently overlooked during inspection of a home is the adequacy of electrical outlets and switches in every room. It is very expensive to route wire inside walls, ceilings, and floors—either to establish new outlets or to install more convenient switches—after construction has been completed. Locate each electrical outlet on your scale drawing in red pencil, and then analyze the adequacy of the total system for your needs.

HEATING SYSTEMS

In certain parts of the United States, gas and electricity are relatively cheap and in plentiful supply. In other areas, however, gas and electricity are the last energy sources to consider for heating. Therefore, determine the suitability of the fuel used in the house for the area in which you will live.

In newly constructed housing, it is probably not necessary to have a heating company inspect the heating system. But in older structures, it is wise to have a professional evaluate the system for any hidden, needed repairs. Moreover, a qualified heating specialist might be able to suggest alterations that could significantly reduce the yearly fuel bill. In such a case, the expense of repairs would be recouped in a short period of time.

Remember, fuel will be a major component in the monthly costs of running a house. Try to get an estimate of what the yearly fuel costs have been and what they will be in the near future. Also, if you are on a limited budget and purchasing a development home in a tropical climate, consider whether you even need the added expense of a heating system.

In the following pages, several common types of heating systems are described so that you may become familiar with their benefits and disadvantages.

1. In **gravity warm-air systems,** the furnace utilizes the fact that warm air is lighter than cold, so hot air rises and cold air settles. The heat rises through ducts and passes through registers into various rooms.

Pro

- This is an easy system in which to install central air conditioning (see p. 65).
- There are no large, exposed radiators.

Con

- There must be a considerable difference in temperature between rising hot air and descending cold air to obtain good air movement.
- Many people complain that it dries out their sinuses and throats.

2. In **hot-water systems,** water is heated and then employed as the medium for transmitting heat principally by a gravity system or a forced hot-water system. (See Fig. 4.6.)

Pro

- This method is generally less drying for those suffering from sinus trouble.

Con

- It requires large radiators or convectors, which take up wall and floor space.

3. In **radiant systems,** heat generated by hot water is conveyed to pipes, which are hidden in surfaces such as floors and ceilings. These surfaces then radiate energy in automatically controlled amounts.

Pro

- Heat sources are invisible—no radiators, convector cabinets, or grills are apparent.

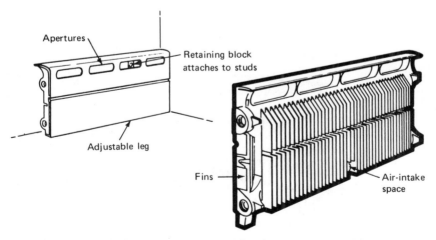

Fig. 4.6. Cast-iron baseboard for hot water or steam.

- Radiant systems can be used to warm basementless homes when other types of heat cannot completely warm the floors.

Con

- Large pieces of furniture and carpeting can intercept the heat.

4. In **steam systems,** water is heated in the boiler until it turns to steam and rises through pipes to radiators. As the steam contacts the radiators, it condenses and returns to the boiler to be reheated. (See Fig. 4.7.)

Pro

- Steam radiators can be smaller than—and yet supply the same heat as—a hot-water system, because steam is hotter than water.
- Steam runs more rapidly through pipes than does hot water, and so a steam system heats up faster.

Con

- The pressure of steam is more dangerous, and more service may be required to operate the system safely.

5. In **electric heat systems,** any electrical conductor with a resistance to electricity will become hot when current is passed through it. Baseboard units are the most popular form. (See Fig. 4.8.)

Pro

- Electrical systems have no moving parts to wear out, and thus are virtually maintenance-free.
- Fuel does not have to be delivered or stored.
- There is no combustion, and thus no expensive chimney need be installed.

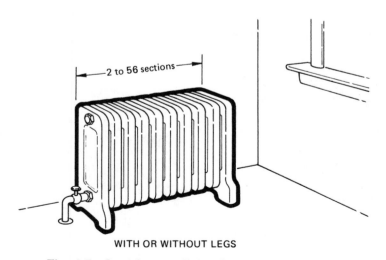

WITH OR WITHOUT LEGS

Fig. 4.7. Cast-iron radiator for water or steam.

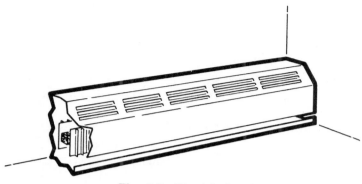

Fig. 4.8. Electric heater.

Con

- In some places, the high cost of electric power makes this type of heating too expensive to be practical.

6. In **solar heating systems,** the energy of the sun is used to heat water, which may be used to heat the home or simply to supply hot water.

Pro

- The fuel source is free.

Con

- Most solar heating systems require a conventional system as a backup for use during sunless periods, thus making the initial cost somewhat higher.
- Finding qualified repair personnel may be difficult.

PLUMBING SYSTEMS

Local building codes regulate the design and materials that may be used in plumbing systems. Check to be certain that the plumbing installed in your potential home conforms to the local code. You can do this either by asking to see a Certificate of Compliance or by calling the local building inspector. Be alert to the quality of the plumbing work. Because plumbing is a major construction cost, how the work is done, and its present condition reflect on the basic value of the house. So, test for pressure in every faucet, and fill the sinks and bathtubs to judge how well they drain. Once you own a house, correcting faulty plumbing work will be an expensive proposition.

Should you be concerned with the type of pipes that supply water? Yes. The following list describes what to look for in four different types:

1. **Steel,** a common type of piping, is found in older structures. It cannot be bent to make turns and thus requires numerous fittings (however, this allows easy replacement). Over time, steel pipes rust, and so, when the water is first turned

on, it may appear brownish for the first few moments. Rust can also accumulate inside steel pipes and reduce the waterflow to certain facilities.

Pitfalls

- When inspecting, check to see if pipes appear rusty on the outside. Such pipes may have to be replaced.
- Test the water pressure of every bathtub, shower, sink, and toilet.

2. **Copper** piping is more expensive than steel and is often used to replace rusted steel pipes. It is very common throughout newer houses. It is easily bent to make turns, and thus there are fewer fittings in a copper system. Since copper joints are usually sweat-soldered, they cannot be unscrewed to replace a damaged pipe. Copper offers less resistance to waterflow, and more pressure is delivered at the tap.

Pitfall

- Most copper pipes cannot be serviced with a pair of open-end wrenches, and so repair costs are higher.

3. **Plastic** piping is generally used for cold-water supply, and most local codes prevent its use within walls. It is the least expensive type of plumbing—a fact that you should consider when you evaluate the overall construction of a house.

Pitfalls

- Plastic piping is the least desirable plumbing system because it is difficult to service and is easily damaged.
- In the event of a fire, some plastic piping gives off harmful fumes.

4. **Brass,** the most expensive and least common piping, is primarily used in areas with severe water problems. Brass pipe is rigid and must be joined and

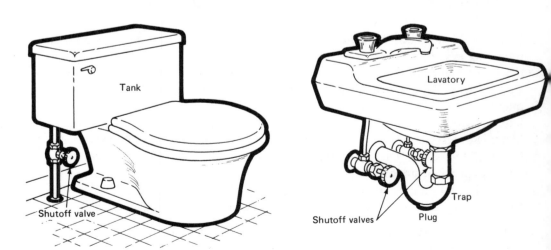

Fig. 4.9. Shutoff valves.

threaded in the same manner as steel pipe. As a general rule, although brass plumbing reflects a high-quality construction job, it adds so much cost that it should only be used where absolutely necessary. The more common copper piping should perform just as satisfactorily where water problems do not exist.

Ideally, each sink, bathtub, shower, water heater, washing machine, and toilet should have its own shutoff valve (see Fig. 4.9). Then, if an emergency arises, you can close off the flow of water to a specific area and still use the rest of the plumbing system. So be sure to check for adequate shutoff valves during the inspection.

INSPECTING THE KITCHEN

One of the most important assets of a home is a functional kitchen. A fully equipped, modern kitchen in the house you buy will be important to the comfort of your family. In addition, it is often a primary attraction to buyers should you later wish to sell.

Some buyers prefer to purchase a house with an outdated kitchen and then to modernize it to their own taste. The cost of complete renovations, however, ranges from $4000 to $10,000. So, if you don't plan on doing that much work, look at the following features during the inspection:

1. *Cabinets*
   ☐ What materials are they made of? Metal cabinets are cheaper than wood and less attractive to most people.

☐ Are they well surfaced and easy to clean? or discolored and in need of recoating with Formica or repainting?

☐ Are the shelves deep enough to accommodate dishes lying flat? Depth should be at least 13 inches.

☐ Is there sufficient storage space for food, pots, dishes, and small appliances?

☐ Are cabinets conveniently located?

2. *Countertops*

☐ How high are the countertops? In most kitchens, 36 inches is the standard height.

☐ Do they have splash guards?

☐ Are there convenient electrical outlets for connecting countertop appliances?

☐ Is the Formica self-edged, or is it cheaply edged with metal?

☐ Is there sufficient preparation space (at least 30 inches) near the sink and stove?

☐ What kind of sink is installed? If it is enamel, check for discoloration or chips. Does it drain well?

3. *Floor*

☐ Is it easy to care for, or will it require constant waxing?

☐ Are there holes, scratches, or tears?

☐ Is the floor level?

4. *Layout*

☐ Is the overall layout awkward?

☐ Is the cooking range vented to remove cooking odors and moisture?

☐ Are there one or more windows?

☐ Are working and eating areas adequately lit?

☐ When opened, does the refrigerator door block other areas?

☐ Is it an eat-in kitchen?

5. *Appliances*

☐ Does the kitchen have the appliances you normally need?

☐ Is the oven built-in? Is it too high for convenient access?

☐ Do the appliances run on electricity or gas? Which do you prefer?

When you are buying a house that has not yet been built, look carefully at the models of kitchen appliances that will be supplied. If they are not satisfactory, offer to pay the developer for the appliances you desire. It is far simpler to do such work in the beginning than to change major appliances at a later date.

AIR CONDITIONING

The two basic types of air conditioning are *central* and *room*. Central air conditioning cools a major portion of a house from a central cooling unit. Room air conditioners cool only the area in which they are placed. There are pluses and minuses to each type.

It costs more to operate central air conditioning than room units because it cools larger areas. However, in most warmer areas of the country, central air conditioning is a valuable part of the purchase price. Central air conditioning is expensive to install because ducts must be run from the central unit to all areas of the house that are to be cooled. Obviously, a house with gravity warm-air heating makes installation easier because most of the ducts are already in place. Central air conditioning can be added to an existing house without forced-air heating. However, this involves major construction work because ducts are usually run inside walls, which, of course, is a major expense.

Room air conditioners allow selection of the particular area to be cooled. They can be built into the wall for aesthetic purposes or set in a window. On the other hand, room units tend to be noisier than central systems. In addition, because parts eventually wear out, room air conditioners involve greater upkeep expenses.

Table 4.1. Proper cooling capacity.

	Btu	Area (in ft^2)
Small capacity (115/120-volt circuit)	3,600	150
	4,800	200
	6,000	250
	7,200	300
	8,400	350
	9,600	400
Large capacity (230/240-volt circuit)	10,800	450
	12,000	500
	13,200	550
	14,400	600
	15,600	650
	16,800	700
	18,000	750
	19,200	800
	20,400	850
	21,600	900
	22,800	950
	24,000	1,000
	25,200	1,050
	26,400	1,100
	27,600	1,150
	28,800	1,200
	30,000	1,250
	31,200	1,300
	32,400	1,350
	33,600	1,400
	34,800	1,450
	36,000	1,500

One way developers can cut costs in the construction of new homes is to put in a smaller type of unit than is adequate for proper cooling. So, before you buy a house with room air conditioning, be certain that the performance of each unit as measured in Btu's is adequate. This is simple to check. Use the floor plan (see p. 46) to compute the floor area of each room in square feet. Then refer to Table 4.1 to find the number of Btu a cooling unit needs to do the job.

WINDOWS

When inspecting a private house, open and close all of the windows. Take note of broken panes of glass and windows that do not close properly. Give the house a plus if it has either double-pane thermal windows, which provide excellent insulation in cold months, or storm windows, which do the same. Don't forget to look for window screens, which are needed during the warmer months. If you don't see them, ask.

The most prevalent type of window is the *double-hung window,* which has an upper portion that slides down and a lower portion that slides up (Fig. 4.10). The frame is sometimes made of aluminum, although in most windows it is wooden.

Fig. 4.10. Double-hung window.

Fig. 4.11. Casement window.

A very common problem is that these windows are often painted shut by careless painters. In an old house where many coats of paint have been applied, it may be impossible to open such a window without damaging it. Another problem is that the sash cord is made of rope, which becomes rotten or frayed over time. Such sash cords must be replaced to allow proper ventilation, as well as escape in case of fire.

Casement windows have metal frames and are hung on hinges at either side of the window frame (Fig. 4.11). They are sometimes opened and closed via operation of a crank. (Be certain that all cranking mechanisms work!) The main problem with casement windows is that they rust and are eventually ruined if not properly painted. If casement windows are in an older house, there may be a draft due to uneven fit of the closed windows. This will affect heating costs. However, corrective measures can be taken to reduce drafts.

Horizontal sliding windows are constructed of aluminum and move along a fitted track at the top and bottom (Fig. 4.12). They sometimes have nylon guides that reduce friction, thus allowing them to operate more smoothly. Cheap horizontal sliding windows will warp and fail to work properly in a short time.

Awning windows are hinged at the top and swing out at the bottom (Fig. 4.13). They are usually operated by a crank or a manual linkage connected to scissors-type metal arms on the window bottom. Be certain that each window fits snugly into the exterior frame so that there are no air leaks. One disadvantage of the awning window is that it may only be opened a certain distance because of the control mechanism.

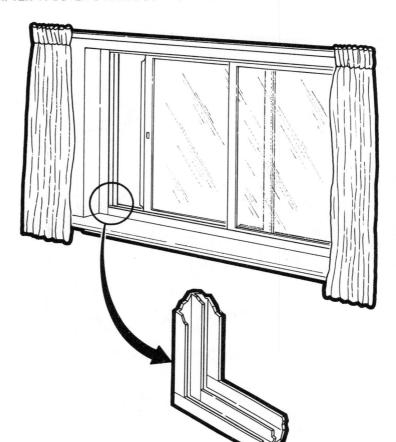

Fig. 4.12. Horizontal sliding windows.

INSULATION

Complete insulation of a house can cut its heat loss from 60% to 70%. Most newer homes are built with fuel savings in mind so that appropriate insulation materials are placed inside walls and between floors during construction. In existing homes, total insulation is not practical, but partial measures can be taken to reduce heat loss. During the inspection, judge the adequacy of insulation through the structure.

Insulating material falls into four general categories: *rigid boards, flexible batts* (also called *blankets*), *loose fill,* and *reflective* (see Fig. 4.14). These materials trap warm air pockets inside them and prevent heat passage from the inside of the house to the outside. Loose-fill insulation is installed in existing houses by drilling a hole through the inner wall and blowing it in by machine. It is an expensive undertaking, and you should expect to pay the seller for this valuable work.

Fig. 4.13. Awning window.

Heat rises, so much of its loss occurs through the ceiling and roof. If a house has an attic, it is easy to check for proper insulation in these areas. In warmer climates, keep in mind that proper insulation can significantly reduce air-conditioning costs.

PROFESSIONAL INSPECTORS AND APPRAISERS

In most areas, you can hire professional inspectors and expert appraisers. Inspectors merely look for defects in the physical property, whereas appraisers give an estimate of the current market value of property. Fees for each service range from $25 to $100. The quality of inspectors' opinions varies greatly, and the best precaution against shoddy workmanship and needed repairs is still your own diligent inspection.

Nevertheless, it is a good idea in the stages before signing a contract to hire an appraiser if your bank or other lending institution has not already done so. Most times, an appraiser is automatically engaged before a mortgage is extended. However, if you need to hire your own, they are listed in the Yellow Pages.

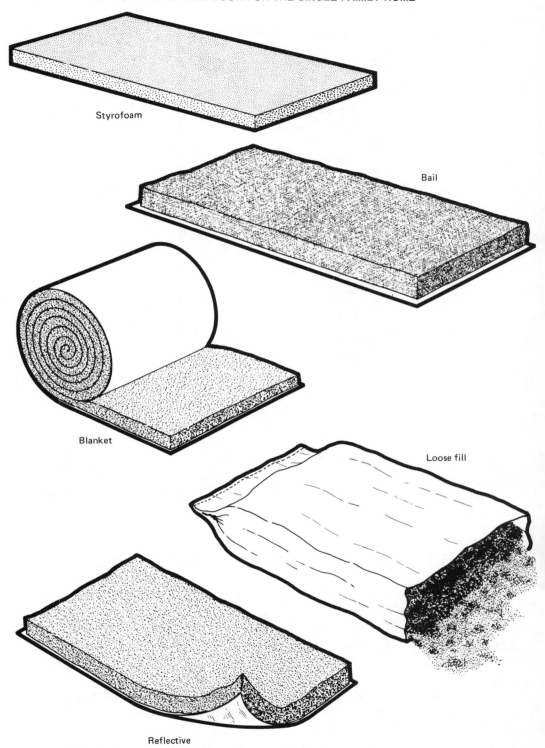

Styrofoam

Bail

Blanket

Loose fill

Reflective

Fig. 4.14. Types of insulation.

5. Negotiating the Purchase

A thing is worth whatever someone is willing and able to pay for it at the time it is sold. Clearly, buyers are in an inherently better position than sellers. Buyers can determine what they are willing to pay, whereas sellers can only attempt to be paid a target sales price that does not exceed the abilities and interest of their potential customers.

When you are making as large an investment as buying a house, use your position as the buyer to your advantage. Your negotiating success failure can mean thousands of dollars on the purchase price. This in turn affects the amount of the down payment and the net monthly cost. Although it is impossible to discuss the entire art of negotiating in this chapter, below are some helpful hints for your strategy:

Rule 1

Fix the maximum price that you will pay, and stick to it. Don't agree immediately to pay the price the seller is asking. It is customary for a seller to add 5% to 10% to the minimum satisfactory price in anticipation of negotiating downward. Make your bid lower than this, and anticipate having to move upward. But never go beyond the maximum price you fixed in the beginning.

Rule 2

Don't discuss your whole strategy with the broker. Brokers make commissions from completing sales, and they may not always keep a confidence. Don't take it for granted that a broker is correct when he or she states that the seller will not accept less than a particular price.

Rule 3

Supply the broker with a sales pitch to give the seller. Explain to the broker the major flaws you have found during your exterior and interior inspection of the house. Never debate these flaws with the broker. Simply tell the broker to inform the seller that these flaws make your bid quite reasonable.

Rule 4

Find out how much the seller paid for the house—and when. This information is almost always available from local mortgages that have been recorded. Most brokers can supply you with the price the seller paid, but will do so only if you ask. Once you know the extent of the seller's profit, you will have a notion of his or her flexibility. For example, a seller who purchased a home six years ago for $35,000, and who is asking $80,000 for it now, is apt to be flexible. On the other hand, a seller who paid $55,000 for a house two years ago, spent $5000 on a finished basement, and is asking $68,500 now, may only be slightly flexible.

Rule 5

Never argue with the seller. You'll lose your advantage if insignificant points turn into matters of honor. If the seller says a new refrigerator-freezer cost $1000 but you know from experience that it should only cost $500, be silent. Make a mental note of it, and take the real cost into account when you are formulating your bid. Sellers are attached to where they live and want to sell their house to someone who appears to appreciate their efforts.

Rule 6

Be businesslike. Don't exhibit undue enthusiasm. This does not mean that you should appear to be as hard as stone. It does mean that you should not make too many positive statements in earshot of the seller. Such statements only encourage the seller to be less flexible because you seem so eager. Appear to be interested—but only at the right price.

Rule 7

Think everything through overnight. It is amazing how tired one can become during serious negotiations. When you are tired, your mind is not at its best. Try to "sleep on" a proposed counteroffer, and ignore the pressuring of brokers or sellers who insist that there are other buyers waiting.

Rule 8

Don't bring along children if you are going to discuss purchasing terms with the seller. Children can be a great distraction. They may pressure you, and they may make encouraging comments to the seller, thus making the seller less flexible. For instance, the seller will recognize that the buyers want to please their three-year-old son who loves the basement gameroom.

Rule 9

Accommodate the seller's needs at the right price. If a seller must move quickly and you can take possession rapidly, use it as a bargaining chip. Likewise, if the seller wishes to remain for several months, use it to your advantage. The seller may choose to accept your bid over a slightly higher bidder who won't meet the seller's imediate needs.

Rule 10

Try to include expensive improvements in the sale price. A seller will often include wall-to-wall carpeting, custom-made furniture, and certain appliances in the sale price, if you ask. If not, you can probably purchase them from the seller at a fraction of their replacement cost because of the expense of moving them.

Rule 11

Find out why the seller is moving. In most cases, a seller has a logical reason for wanting to move. If the reason seems farfetched, however, or if you don't think it fits the seller's circumstances, investigate. This may be your tip-off that something is wrong with the house or with the real-estate market in the area. On the other hand, it may be your tip-off that the seller has an urgent need to move quickly and will accept a lower price.

Rule 12

Buy in late fall if you possibly can. In many parts of the country, the price of shelter peaks in spring and dips lowest in late fall. One reason is that most families want their children settled in a new school before the end of September. Thus, by late fall, many once-potential buyers have purchased their house. When sellers see fewer potential customers, they may develop a sense of urgency—especially in areas where the winter is quite severe. Spring, on the other hand, marks the beginning of a long selling season, and buyers may feel then that they can afford to wait for their price.

ALLOWING A LAWYER TO NEGOTIATE

If your own skills as a negotiator are not particularly effective, consider allowing an attorney to negotiate the purchase. Most attorneys have experience in real estate as well as in negotiating contracts. Moreover, there are several subtle advantages to having a third party negotiate with the seller. First, a third party must always consult the actual buyer before agreeing to any offer the seller proposes. This time lag gives the buyer an opportunity for reflection and helps prevent hasty decisions. Second, the buyer gains the insight of an objective observer who is not tied up in the emotion of desiring a particular house.

6. Legal Considerations

SELECTING A LAWYER

You should engage a competent lawyer *before* making the final decision to purchase. Many lawyers are experienced in real-estate transactions, so their opinion of what you are buying is valuable. Provide the lawyer with all of the research data from the worksheets so that he or she can act as an independent adviser as well as a legal representative. The more local the attorney is, the more likely it is that he or she will be familiar with the particular area in which you intend to purchase a house.

It is now relatively easy to find a good lawyer. Most local bar associations have an attorney reference service. In addition, lawyers may now advertise so you might want to check local newspapers. Don't forget to interview your prospective lawyer regarding his or her experience and knowledge in real estate. Ask what percentage of the lawyer's practice is in real estate, what bank or real-estate broker references can be furnished, and previous transactions in the community.

Generally, legal fees for a completed transaction run from 0.5% to 1% of the purchase price. This number may go higher if there are complications with title that need to be corrected. Once you feel comfortable with an attorney, establish a fee and be certain you understand what will be done for it. Sometimes, it is best to divide the fee into two parts: one for drawing up the contract of sale and giving advice, and the other for completing the closing. This is because there will be uncertainty that a final purchase can be accomplished. Such events as hidden defects in title or your failure to qualify for a mortgage could prevent the final passing of title.

Don't sign anything without first consulting your lawyer. Remember that skimping on legal counsel is often the first step to disaster. It is much easier to prevent blundering into trouble than to clear up needlessly created difficulties.

The following text discusses some of the legal matters that come up during the transfer of homeownership. Study them to prepare yourself for what will take place when you buy a house. Also, refer to the Glossary of General Terms (pp. 127–135) to clarify any terminology that seems confusing.

BINDERS

Binders are forms that are prepared by brokers who wish to lock up a transaction on a particular home (see Exhibit 6.1). Avoid signing a binder if you possibly can. Many real-estate brokers prepare a binder that sets forth enough details (i.e., price, parties, date) of the proposed sale that a court may enforce the binder as though it were a contract. In such cases, the parties to the sale are deprived of any opportunity to include necessary language to protect their individual interests. Therefore, if the seller and broker insist that you sign a binder, put them off until you have shown it to your attorney.

LIENS

A *lien* is a legal claim on another's property as security for a debt. Most liens arise out of the time, efforts, or goods expended by laborers, mechanics, or material suppliers in repairing or financing property. Since a creditor has a right to have his or her debt satisfied, the failure to pay sums owed may bring about a legal power to sell the debtor's house to raise the money. So a lien is a threat to ownership and

EXHIBIT 6.1

BINDER AGREEMENT

Date...19........

Received from ....

of ....

the sum of .... Dollars

as deposit on account of purchase price of premises ....

.... N. Y.

on the following terms and conditions:

TERMS:

Purchase Price is $..payable as follows:

$............................(including above deposit) on the signing of the formal contract as hereinafter provided.

$............................by taking title subject to a first mortgage in that amount covering said premises, bearing interest at the rate of............% per annum payable....................annually, principal due.........................

....

$............................by taking title subject to a second mortgage in that amount covering said premises, bearing interest at the rate of ....% per annum payable....................annually, prin.ipal due...............................

....

$............................by the purchaser or assigns executing and delivering to the seller on delivery of the deed a purchase money bond and...............................mortgage in that amount covering said premises, bearing interest at the rate of............% per annum payable....................annually, principal due.......................................

....

$............................ , the balance, in cash or certified check on delivery of deed.

CONDITIONS:

This deposit is accepted subject to owner's approval of the terms and conditions. If such approval is not obtained on or before five days from date hereof, this deposit shall be repaid to purchaser, but if obtained within such period a more formal contract in the form used by

shall be signed by the parties at the office of ....at No. ....

....at.................m., on..19........

The deed shall be delivered on the....................day of..........................19......., at...............M. at the office of

....

SUBJECT to rights of tenants as follows: ....

....

SUBJECT, also, to the following: ....

....

....

....

The parties agree that ....

as broker brought about this sale and the seller agrees to pay the usual brokerage commission.

This agreement may not be changed orally, but only by an agreement in writing and signed by the party against whom enforcement of any waiver, change, modification or discharge is sought.

The above terms and conditions are approved
and receipt of above deposit is acknowledged.

....
Broker.

....
Owner.

I agree to the foregoing.

....
Purchaser.

may therefore render title unmarketable. The most common types of liens are mortgage, tax, mechanic, and judgment.

When you buy a house, you will probably have to finance a major portion of the purchase price. Several *instruments* will be executed to assure repayment. One will be a *promissory note* (in some states called a *bond*), which is evidence of the debt. This is a personal liability that will be enforceable no matter where you live. The other instrument will be a *mortgage,* which pledges to the lender your specific house as collateral. Therefore, until you repay the lender, there will be a mortgage lien on the house. Such liens are filed at the county clerk's office to give all potential purchasers notice that the property is collateral for a debt. A title search includes an investigation for filed mortgage liens.

According to the law, whenever a tax is levied on a specific piece of real property, it becomes a *tax lien*. Once the tax is paid, the lien is removed and the title again becomes free and clear. A homeowner's failure to pay property or other taxes empowers the government to foreclose on the property and sell it to satisfy all taxes due. A buyer should be certain that the seller has paid all such tax liens, or he or she may become liable for the debt.

A *mechanic's lien* is a security claim given by statute to one who improves real property. Workers have the right to receive compensation for adding value to a house. Generally, a mechanic's lien is filed as a notice in the county clerk's office. If it goes unsatisfied, then a foreclosure may be brought to collect the amount due. Once the improvements have been paid for, a *certificate of satisfaction* is issued to acknowledge payment. Mechanic's liens are checked by the title searcher to assure a purchaser that no claims that are properly filed pass with the property to the new owner.

A *judgment lien* arises out of a successful lawsuit or other legal proceeding. It may originate in either a state or federal court. Once again, the property may be sold against the owner's will by an officer of the court in order to collect sums due under the judgment. Since this type of lien arises from a lawsuit, the debtor must receive some notice of the pending legal action. In court, the merits of the parties were considered, and the outcome decided by a judge or jury. What is important is that the lien itself affects marketability of title, which is ultimately reflected in the value of the house. You don't have to be an expert in liens before buying a house. Your lawyer should check these matters for you when ordering a title search. But you should be able to decide, with the help of your attorney, whether a particular lien is serious enough to renegotiate or stop the purchase.

EASEMENTS

An *easement* is the right of one party to enjoy certain uses of property belonging to another. For example, a house built behind the house adjacent to the street may have a driveway running over the front house's property. Power, water, or drainage lines running across another's land are other common easements.

Easements are expressly created in written agreements, arise out of necessity, or are acquired by long use. Easements acquired by continued use are the most difficult to discover before purchase. Each state has its own period of time for continuous use, and most range from 10 to 20 years. The owner must act to prohibit the use, or the claim will become incontestable. For example, if a proper survey shows that a neighbor's driveway is partly on property about to be purchased, the buyer must act to have it removed. If no action is taken in the proscribed time, an easement will arise that allows the driveway to remain on the buyer's land.

If you suspect a wall, walkway, driveway, patio, garden, or other encroachment is on your prospective land, consult a recent survey of the property. However, some easements, such as those for utility or telephone companies, are a necessity and should cause little concern. In the written title report, disclosure will be made of all easements that have been recorded. If there is a use you don't understand, ask your attorney to explain it. Remember that the right of a third party to use your land will be reflected in the marketability of your house.

PUBLIC LIMITATIONS ON OWNER'S RIGHTS

In general, a municipality may acquire land for public use through *eminent domain*. This may occur through outright purchase or obtaining an easement over privately held land for widening a street, laying sewer lines, or other public purpose. This does not always reduce the value of the land. However, it may disrupt the aesthetics of the property or decrease the desirability of the location. In such cases, this will be reflected in a lower sales price.

It is difficult to predict the possibility of such public incursions on a particular property. For instance, in areas where flood control is a problem and drainage is poor, these problems are likely to be corrected. In such circumstances, the benefit to a homeowner may outweigh any inconvenience. On the other hand, beware of houses on heavily trafficked streets that are narrow and full of curves. At some point, the municipality might widen and straighten them. This could bring about the condemnation of part of your land and also place your house closer to street noises.

SOME WORDS ABOUT TITLE

The owner of land has the legal right—or *title*—to its possession. Title also confers upon the owner recourse to legal power to defend the property against the unjust intrusions of others. Thus, a new homeowner would want a title that has no restrictions on normal use and enjoyment. Hidden easements, zoning, restrictive covenants, or a defective deed somewhere in a previous owner cast doubt on the quality of title. So be aware of any such problems *before* making the purchase.

TITLE SEARCH

The primary purpose of fixing a closing date some weeks or months in the future in the Contract of Sale is to search the title. The buyer's attorney will hire a title company to find out if there are any restrictions on the property or house. The inspections are made by an expert who is qualified to recognize problems. A title search report is sent to the attorney who will read it and advise the buyer of potential problems. Exhibit 6.2 is a sample of such a title search.

Even a reasonably thorough title search can fail to discover certain defects in title, such as forgery. Therefore, the attorney will usually advise the buyer to purchase a title insurance policy to guard against these hidden risks. In fact, many lending institutions require that buyers obtain such insurance for the amount of the mortgage so they can be certain there are no problems with their security. Buyers should also insure the purchase amount belonging to them (i.e., the down payment). In this way, if some defect is discovered with their title, they will not lose the down payment and can use these funds to purchase another house.

DEEDS

A *deed* is a document that gives evidence of ownership of real estate. There are three main types of deeds: deed with full covenant, bargain-and-sale deed, and quitclaim deed.

The *deed with full covenant* (frequently called a *warranty deed*) contains the seller's representation that he or she owns the property, has the right to sell it, and that there are no defects in title. This is the most desirable type of deed since it gives the buyer broad assurances backed by the seller. Failure of any covenant gives the buyer the right to sue the seller for damages.

EXHIBIT 6.2
SAMPLE TITLE SEARCH
REPORT

CERTIFICATE OF TITLE

THE TITLE GUARANTEE COMPANY
(A NEW YORK CORPORATION)

and

PIONEER NATIONAL TITLE INSURANCE COMPANY
(A CALIFORNIA CORPORATION) TOGETHER HEREIN CALLED "THE COMPANY"

No. 7099999

Certifies to   Abel, Baker and Charles, Esqs.
100 First Avenue
Staten Island, New York 10300

OFFICE COPY

SPECIMEN: PREPARED FOR INSTRUCTIONAL PURPOSES ONLY

that an examination of title to the premises described in Schedule A has been made in accordance with its usual procedure and agrees to issue its standard form of insurance policy in the amount of $ 45,000.00   insuring A FEE TITLE   and the marketability thereof, after the closing of the transaction in conformance with procedures approved by the Company excepting (a) all loss or damage by reason of the estates, interests, defects, objections, liens, incumbrances and other matters set forth herein that are not disposed of to the satisfaction of the Company prior to such closing or issuance of the policy (b) any question or objection coming to the attention of the Company before the date of closing, or if there be no closing, before the issuance of said policy.

This Certificate shall be null and void (1) if the fees therefor are not paid (2) if the prospective insured, his attorney or agent makes any untrue statement with respect to any material fact or suppresses or fails to disclose any material fact or if any untrue answers are given to material inquiries by or on behalf of the Company (3) upon delivery of the policy. Any claim arising by reason of the issuance hereof shall be restricted to the terms and conditions of the standard form of insurance policy. If title, interest or lien to be insured was acquired by the prospective insured prior to delivery hereof, the Company assumes no liability except under its policy when issued.

THIS CERTIFICATE IS INTENDED FOR LAWYERS ONLY. SUCH EXCEPTIONS AS MAY BE SET FORTH HEREIN MAY AFFECT MARKETABILITY OF TITLE. YOUR LAWYER SHOULD BE CONSULTED BEFORE TAKING ANY ACTION BASED UPON THE CONTENTS HEREOF. THE COMPANY'S REPRESENTATIVE AT THE CLOSING HEREUNDER MAY NOT ACT AS LEGAL ADVISOR TO ANY OF THE PARTIES OR DRAW LEGAL INSTRUMENTS FOR THEM. SUCH REPRESENTATIVE IS PERMITTED TO BE OF ASSISTANCE ONLY TO AN ATTORNEY. IT IS ADVISABLE TO HAVE YOUR ATTORNEY PRESENT AT THE CLOSING.

IF ANY OF THE CLOSING INSTRUMENTS WILL BE OTHER THAN COMMONLY USED FORMS OR CONTAIN UNUSUAL PROVISIONS, THE CLOSING CAN BE SIMPLIFIED AND EXPEDITED BY FURNISHING THE COMPANY WITH COPIES OF THE PROPOSED DOCUMENTS IN ADVANCE OF CLOSING.

Dated 9 A.M. November 15, 1977   Premises in Section 9   Block 10001
Redated 9 A.M.   on land map of County of

Joseph Clearer, Esq.   THE TITLE GUARANTEE COMPANY
and
(212) 964-1000   PIONEER NATIONAL TITLE INSURANCE COMPANY
*Will be pleased to confer on any
questions concerning this certificate*

MEMBERS NEW YORK BOARD OF TITLE UNDERWRITERS   CERTIFIED BY

See Over Page for General Exceptions from Coverage

IF THE INSURED CONTEMPLATES MAKING IMPROVEMENTS TO THE PROPERTY COSTING MORE THAN TWENTY PER CENTUM OF THE AMOUNT OF INSURANCE TO BE ISSUED HEREUNDER, WE SUGGEST THAT THE AMOUNT OF INSURANCE BE INCREASED TO COVER THE COST THEREOF; OTHERWISE, IN CERTAIN CASES THE INSURED WILL BECOME A CO-INSURER.

The following estates, interests, defects, objections to title, liens and incumbrances and other matters are excepted from the coverage of our standard form of policy:

1. Defects and incumbrances arising or becoming a lien after the date of this policy.

2. Consequences of the exercise and enforcement or attempted enforcement of any governmental war or police powers over the premises.

3. Any laws, regulations or ordinances (including, but not limited to zoning, building, and environmental protection) as to use, occupancy, subdivision or improvement of the premises adopted or imposed by any governmental body, or the effect of any noncompliance with or any violation thereof.

4. Judgments against the insured or estates, interests, defects, objections, liens or incumbrances created, suffered, assumed or agreed to by or with the privity of the insured.

5. Title to any property beyond the lines of the premises, or title to areas within or rights or easements in any abutting streets, roads, avenues, lanes, ways or waterways, or the right to maintain therein vaults, tunnels, ramps or any other structure or improvement, unless this policy specifically provides that such titles, rights, or easements are insured. Notwithstanding any provisions in this paragraph to the contrary, this policy, unless otherwise excepted, insures the ordinary rights of access and egress belonging to abutting owners.

6. Title to any personal property, whether the same be attached to or used in connection with said premises or otherwise.

Our policy will except from coverage any state of facts which an accurate survey might show, unless survey coverage is ordered. When such coverage is ordered, this certificate will set forth the specific survey exceptions which we will include in our policy. Whenever the word "trim" is used in any survey exceptions from coverage, it shall be deemed to include, roof cornice, show window cornice, lintels, sills, window trim, entrance trim, bay window cornices, mouldings, belt courses, water tables, keystones, pilasters, portico, balcony all of which project beyond the street line.

In certain areas, our policy will except from coverage any state of facts which a personal inspection might disclose unless survey coverage is ordered. In these cases a specific exception will appear in this certificate.

Our examination of the title includes a search for any unexpired financing statements which affect fixtures and which have been properly filed and indexed pursuant to the Uniform Commercial Code in the office of the recording officer of the county in which the real property lies.

No search has been made for other financing statements because we do not insure title to personal property. We will on request, in connection with the issuance of a title insurance policy, prepare such search for an additional charge. Our liability in connection with such search is limited to $1,000.00.

THIS COMPANY CERTIFIES that a good and marketable title to the premises described in Schedule A subject to the liens, incumbrances and other matters, if any, set forth in this certificate may be by:

MARY SELLER

> Deed made by John Priorowner to John Seller and Mary Seller, his wife, dated February 15, 1974, recorded February 17, 1974, in Reel 119 at page 123.

Source of title

> 1½ story frame dwelling, garage in rear; common driveway on south, Mr. & Mrs. John Tenant in possesion, as lessees, claim option to purchase.

Inspection discloses

Inspection Dated: November 1, 1977

We set forth the additional matters which will appear in our policy as exceptions from coverage, unless disposed of to our satisfaction prior to the closing or delivery of the policy.

1. Taxes, tax liens, tax sales, water rates, sewer rents and assessments set forth herein.
2. Mortgages returned herewith and set forth herein. (Two   )

INSERT NUMBER

3. Any state of facts which an accurate survey might show.
4. Survey exceptions set forth herein.
5. Affidavit of Title will be required on closing.
6. Compliance with the Federal "Truth in Lending Act".

There are no restrictive covenants, conditions or easements of record unless set forth immediately following.

A. Covenants and Restrictions in Liber 2111 cp 333, the 2 story requirement of which may be violated by the 1½ story dwelling on the premises, but this policy insures that said building may remain undisturbed so long as it stands.

B. Guaranteed survey made by G. Stakeout. Licensed Surveyor, dated January 15, 1935 shows a semiattached 1½ story dwelling; also shows:
   1) The northerly wall is a party wall;
   2) A common driveway on the south;
   3) Retaining wall along easterly line encroaches on premises adjoining on the east by as much as 0.5 feet;
   4) The owner is out of possession of a strip of land having a maximum width of 1.6 feet lying north of the northerly fence, for a distance of approximately 20 feet. Title to said strip is not insured.
   5) Garage on premises described in Schedule "A" encroaches on premises adjoining on the east up to 0.3 feet, but this policy insures that the encroaching wall may remain as long as said building stands;
   6) Garage erected on premises adjoining on the south encroaches up to 0.6 feet on the premises described in Schedule "A";
   7) Encroachments on Locust Street;
      (a) Steps up to 2.0 feet.
      (b) Hedges up to 3 feet more or less;
   8) Proposed widening of Locust Street affecting the westerly 5 feet of our premises (See Exception "C");
   9) Any state of facts an accurate survey might show since survey made by Good Stakeout, dated January 15, 1935.

C. Approximately 5 feet of the premises described in Schedule "A" lies in the bed of Locust Street as the same is laid out on the Official Map of the City of New York. This portion of the premises is subject to the restricted use imposed by the provisions of Section 35 of the General City Law.

(continued)

MF   Title No. 7099999

Additional Exceptions

D. Rights of tenants, if any.

E. Unrecorded lease of John Tenant and wife, purportedly containing an option to purchase, as disclosed by inspection report.

F. The following must be disposed of:

(1) JUDGMENT: Supreme Court, Richmond County
   Perf: March 30, 1975; Docketed March 30, 1975
   Amount $9600.00; Atty.: I. Ketcham and U. Ketcham, 123 East Street, New York, N.Y.
      Debtor: John A. Seller and Mary Seller, both of 55 West Street, New York, N.Y.
      Creditor: A.B.C. Finance Corp., 120 Broadway, New York, N.Y.

(2) FEDERAL TAX LIEN vs. Mary Seller in the amount of $465.00, filed April 3, 1973, Number 56541—Income Tax 1971.

G. Lis Pendens filed on January 17, 1976, Number 196—1976, Top Roofing Corp. vs. John Seller, et al. to foreclose mechanic's lien filed 4/15/75; Plaintiff's attorney—Harvey Helper, Esq.

H. Mechanic's Lien filed by Top Roofing Corp. against John Seller, owner on April 15, 1975, amount $750.00.

I. U.C.C. #9436 filed by Sizzle Burner Corp. against John Seller and Mary Seller on September 15, 1975, for the sum of $1200.00 covers oil burner, etc.

J. The Deed from John Priorowner to John Seller and Mary Seller, his wife, dated 2/15/74, recorded 2/17/74, in Reel 119 at Page 123 recites:
   "Being the same premises conveyed to the party of the first part by Deed from Pauline Priorowner, dated 1/20/70, recorded 1/20/70, in Reel 105, page 200."
Said Deed recorded in Reel 105, page 200 only conveyed an undivided one-half interest in the premises under examination to John Priorowner.
   A Deed is required from John Priorowner covering the undivided one-half interest and still outstanding in him by reason of the aforementioned recital.

K. Franchise Tax Due against Hot Properties, Inc.—report from Albany dated 2/8/72—owes tax which became a lien 3/15/69 (Out of title by Deed to Pauline Priorowner, dated 10/15/69, recorded 10/17/69 in Reel 85, Page 12).

L. Possible N.Y. City Corporation Tax due against Hot Properties Inc. to 10/17/69.

M. The Deed from Seymour Sizzler to Sophie Sizzler dated October 31, 1965, acknowledged on October 31, 1965 was not recorded until February 3, 1966 in Liber 5700 cp 400. Satisfactory proof is required showing that said deed was recorded during the lifetime of the grantor therein.

N. Proof is required by affidavit and death certificate showing the death of John Seller, who is purported to have died on December 10, 1975. (No proceedings in Richmond County.)

O. New York and Federal Estate Tax against John Seller, deceased; (died on December 10, 1975, Richmond County)
   This exception will be omitted upon conveyance to a bona fide purchaser for fair value.

P. Debts against the estate of John Seller, deceased.

Q. Power of Attorney from Mary Seller to John Seller, Jr. to be considered and recorded, and proof furnished that the Power will be exercised while donor is alive and under no legal incapacity and that the Power has not been revoked at the moment of closing. (Full consideration must be recited in the Deed).

The closing requirements set forth on the following page are a part of this certificate and must be complied with. A duplicate copy of the exceptions is furnished you with the thought you may wish to transmit, with or without any of the other exceptions in the title report, to the attorney for the owner of the property and thereby facilitate the clearing of the objections prior to closing.

Title No. 7099999

SCHEDULE A

ALL that certain plot, piece or parcel of land, with the buildings thereon erected, situate, lying and being in the City and State of New York, County of Richmond shown and designated as Lots Numbered 21 through 24, both inclusive, all in Block Numbered 35 on a certain map entitled, "Map of Richmond Gardens, situated in the Borough and County of Richmond, State of New York and filed in the Office of the Reigster of the County of Richmond on January 31, 1927 as Map Number 1065, being more particularly bounded and described as follows:

BEGINNING at a point in the easterly side of Locust Street, distant 266.48 feet northerly from the corner formed by the intersection of the easterly line of Locust Street with the northerly line of Bayview Avenue;

RUNNING THENCE easterly at right angles to Locust Street, 150 feet;

THENCE northerly parallel or nearly so with Locust Street, 45.76 feet to the southerly line of property of Dr. Martin J. Dair (sometimes spelled Dare);

THENCE westerly along the southerly line of said Dair's property, 150 feet to the easterly side of Locust Street; and

THENCE southerly along the easterly side of Locust Street, 47.59 feet to the point or place of BEGINNING.

ADD IN DEED OR MORTGAGE BUT OMIT FROM POLICY:

SAID PREMISES known as and by Street Number 30 Locust Place, Richmond County.

For Conveyancing Only
To seller with all right, title and interest of, in and to any streets and roads abutting the above described premises.
Our policies of title insurance include such buildings and improvements thereon which by law constitute real property, unless specifically accepted therein. Now is the time to determine whether we have examined all of the property and easements which you desire to be insured. If there are appurtenant easements to be insured, please request such insurance. In some cases, our rate manual provides for an additional charge for such insurance.

AFFIDAVIT OF TITLE

State of New York, County of   ss.:   Title No._____

being duly sworn says:

I reside at No.

*If owner is a corporation, fill in office held by deponent and name of corporation.

I am the

owner in fee simple of premises

and   the grantee described in a certain deed of said premises recorded in the Registor's Office of   County in Liber   of Conveyances, page

Said premises have been in my possession since 19   ; that my possession thereof has been peaceable and undisturbed, and the title thereto has never been disputed, questioned, or rejected, nor insurance thereon refused, as far as I know. I know of no facts by reason of which said premises or any interest therein adverse to me might be set up. There are no Federal tax claims or liens assessed or filed against me. There are no judgments against me unpaid or unsatisfied of record entered in any court of this state or of the United States, and said premises are, as far as I know, free from all leases, mortgages, taxes, assessment, water charges, sewer rents and other liens and encumbrances, except

Said premises are now occupied by

No proceedings in bankruptcy have ever been instituted by or against me in any court or before any officer of any state, or of the United States, nor have I at any time made an assignment for the benefit of credits, nor an assignment, now in effect, of the rents of said premises or any part thereof.

*This paragraph to be omitted if owner is a corporation.

*I am a citizen of the United States, and am more than 21 years old. I am by occupation   . I am married to   who is over the age of 21 years and is competent to convey or mortgage real estate. I was married to her on the   day of   19   . I have never been married to any other person now living. I have not been known by any other name during the past ten years.

*This paragraph to be omitted if owner is not a corporation.

*That the charter of said corporation is in full force and effect and no proceeding is pending for dissolution or annulment. That all license and franchise taxes due and payable by said corporation have been paid in full.

There are no actions pending said premises. That no repairs, alterations or improvewments have been made to said premises which have not been completed more than four months prior to the date hereof. There are no facts known to me relating to the title to said premises which have not been set forth in this affidavit.

This affidavit is made to induce   to accept a   on said premises, and to induce The Title Guarantee Company and Pioneer National Title Insurance Company hereinafter called ''The Company'' to issue a policy of title insurance numbered above covering said premises knowing that they will rely on the statements herein made.

Sworn to before me this

day of   , 19   _____

These requirements are a part of this Certificate and must be complied with:

I.   IDENTITY OF ALL PERSONS executing the papers delivered on the closing must be established to the satisfaction of this company. Therefore, the affidavit of title which follows must be properly executed.

II.   WIFE OF ANY OWNER must join in executing all deeds, leases and mortgages (except purchase money mortgages) if the title was acquired by the husband and the marriage occurred prior to September 1, 1930. If the title was acquired before that date and the marriage occurred after that date, the date of the marriage and the fact that the husband was not previously married should be set forth in the affidavit of title.

III.   ALL CONTRACTS must be submitted for consideration at or prior to closing of title.

IV.   PROVISIONS of the N.Y. State Stamp Tax Act and, if the premises are located within the City of New York, the provisions of the New York City Real Property Transfer Tax Law must be complied with.

V.   CORPORATIONS
       1. RESOLUTION OF BOARD OF DIRECTORS: A copy of an appropriate resolution of the board of directors must be furnished when a corporation is to execute the deed, mortgage or lease to be insured.
       2. STOCKHOLDER'S CONSENT: Satisfactory proof of consent of all the stockholders in writing or two-thirds at a meeting duly called, must be furnished when a stock corporation is selling, leasing, exchanging or otherwise disposing of its property. Consent of stockholders is not required when a mortgage is made by a corporation unless the certificate of incorporation, a by-law, or a statute creating the corporation requires such consent.

VI.   IN BUILDING LOAN TRANSACTIONS, the contract must be filed as required by the Lien Law and all advances thereunder must be made in accordance with the terms of such contract. All searches should be continued for each advance and the Company notified of the date and amount of each advance. Applicant must decide whether a survey or surveys should be obtained before making any advance, since, in the absence of a new survey or the redating of the existing survey to the date of each advance, the policy in such cases will except any changes which might have occurred since the date of the survey used herein or will except any state of facts which an accurate survey may show, if no survey protection has been ordered.

VII.   ESTOPPEL CERTIFICATES: If an assignment of an existing mortgage or other lien is to be insured proper estoppel certificates executed in recordable form by the *owners of the fee* and of *subsequent encumbrances* must be obtained before the closing of the title.

VIII. FRANCHISE TAXES: If the party certified to execute the closing instruments is a corporation, possible unpaid N. Y. State franchise taxes and N. Y. City corporation taxes becoming liens after the date of this Certificate will be excepted from coverage under our policy. This applies also to a corporation acquiring title after the date of this Certificate and executing any of the closing instruments.

IX. DEED IN LIEU OF FORECLOSURE: Where the Company is asked to insure title to the grantee in a conveyance made to avoid foreclosure or in any other case which does not involve an actual sale of the property, the policy will contain the following exception: "Possibility of the transfer, conveyance or deed being attacked or set aside under the Bankruptcy Law, by reason of a petition in bankruptcy being filed by or against the grantor within one (1) year of the date of recording of said conveyance and any loss or damage from claims or rights, if any, of the creditors of the grantor. This exception may be eliminated only on approval of Counsel after the Company is furnished with satisfactory proof in affidavit form of the solvency of the grantor, the fairness of the transaction and, if the grantor is a corporation, the consent of all stockholders.

X. CONTINUATION OF SEARCHES: This Company must be notified immediately of the recording or the filing, after the date of this Certificate, of any instrument and of the discharge or other disposition of any mortgage, judgment, lien or any other matter set forth in this Certificate and of any change in the transaction to be insured or the parties thereof. The continuation will not otherwise disclose the disposition of any lien.

XI. TRUST CLAUSE: Mortgages must contain the trust clause required by subdivision 3 of Section 13 of the Lien Law and deeds must contain the trust clause required by subdivision 5 of said section.

XII. REFERENCE TO SURVEYS AND MAPS: Closing instruments should make no reference to surveys or maps unless such surveys or maps are on file. The Westchester County Clerk refuses to accept instruments which contain a reference to a survey even in the "subject" clause.

XIII. CAPACITY OF THE INSURED to take, hold, mortgage and convey real property must be considered.

NOTE: ALL PAPERS IN THIS TITLE RECEIVED BY THE COMPANY FOR RECORDATION WILL BE RETURNED DIRECTLY BY THE REGISTER'S OR COUNTY CLERK'S OFFICE.

FORM OF AFFIDAVIT OF TITLE ON REVERSE SIDE.

Title No. 7099999

The unpaid taxes, water rates, assessments and other matters relating to taxes which are liens at the date of this certificate are set forth below.

Our policy does not insure against such items which have not become a lien up to the date of the policy or installments due after the date of the policy. Neither our tax search nor our policy covers any part of streets on which the premises to be insured abut.

If the tax lots above mentioned cover more or less than the premises under examination, this fact will be noted herein.

In such case the interested parties should take the necessary steps to make the tax map conform to the description to be insured.

For information only, we set forth the assessed valuation for the current year: 1975/76

```
                150
LOCUST    47.59          45.76
ST.             150

          266.48
```

BAYVIEW AVE.

Section 9	Block 10001	Lot 3	Land	$12,000.00
			Total	$35,000.00
			Returns	

Disposition   Tax Exemptions ceases immediately upon conveyance by the exempt Veteran, Pensioner or Exempt institution shown hereon and Policy will except "additional taxes to be added retroactively from date of the termination of Exemption."

1977/78	1st	¼	due	8/1/77	$684.50	PAID
	2nd	¼	due	10/1/77	684.50	PAID
	3rd	¼	due	1/1/78	684.50	OPEN
	4th	¼	due	4/1/78	684.50	OPEN

1977/78 Water Tax-$190.00 OPEN

1976 Sewer Rent-$92.50 OPEN

Nothing else to 11/1/77

Recent payments of any open items returned on this tax search may not yet be reflected on the public records.
Therefore please request the seller or borrower to have the receipted bills available at the closing.

The City Collector will not issue receipts for payments made on and after July 1, 1972, on account of taxes, water, sewer rent charges or assessments unless the taxpayer requests a receipt when paying such items.

Immediate receipts will be issued by the Collector if any of such items are paid in person in acceptable money at the City Collector's Counter.

Since it takes approximately six (6) weeks before the official posting of the payment of these items, sellers and mortgagors should be apprised of the foregoing and if necessary receipts will not be available at the closing or if the official records will not reflect payments made, attorney for sellers and mortgagors should communicate with our designated Clearance Officer prior to closing to make appropriate arrangements with us for the mark-off of such open items.

rc   Title No. 7099999

The following mortgage is open of record:

Disposition

Mortgagor	Amount	$1200.
SAMUEL JONES	Dated	12/24/29
	Recorded	12/24/29
	Liber	1678 mp. 89

Mortgagee	Tax	$5. paid
MABEL MONES	Clauses:	30 days interest
		30 days inst. principal
		30 days taxes, and assessments

Due   as per bond.

Interest   as per bond.

Prepayment Privileges
ASSIGNMENT
Assignor: Mabel Mones   Dated 12/20/31
Assignee: Sara Jones   Rec'd 1/3/32
Assigns mortgage in Liber 1678   Liber 1715 mp. 789
mp. 89.

THE ABOVE MORTGAGE   CAN BE SATISFIED OR ASSIGNED BY:

                                     Sara Jones

This mortgage unless it is to be insured, will appear as an exception from coverage. THE INFORMATION SET FORTH HEREIN IS NOT COMPLETE. REFERENCE SHOULD BE MADE TO THE RECORDED INSTRUMENT. Sometimes, the provisions of a mortgage are modified by agreements which are not recorded. We suggest that you communicate with the mortgagee, if you desire any additional information.

If the above mortgage is satisfied before the closing, please notify our Law Department.

rc   Title No. 7099999

The following mortgage is open of record:

Disposition

Mortgagor	Amount	$19,000.00
HOT PROPERTIES, INC.	Dated	3/1/69
	Recorded	3/3/69
	Liber	5550 mp. 330

Mortgagee	Tax	$95.00 PAID
LEADING OF RICHMOND COUNTY	Clauses:	10 days interest
		10 days inst. principal
		10 days taxes, and assessments

Due   MARCH 1, 1990

Interest   6% — Payable quarterly on the 1st days of June,
September, December and March.

Prepayment Privileges
In multiples of $100.00 on any interest date on 30 days notice.
2% prepayment charge within 5 years; 1% thereafter.

THE ABOVE MORTGAGE   CAN BE SATISFIED OR ASSIGNED BY:
Lending Bank of Bronx County

This mortgage unless it is to be insured, will appear as an exception from coverage. THE INFORMATION SET FORTH HEREIN IS NOT COMPLETE. REFERENCE SHOULD BE MADE TO THE RECORDED INSTRUMENT. Sometimes, the provisions of a mortgage are modified by agreements which are not recorded. We suggest that you communicate with the mortgagee, if you desire any additional information.

If the above mortgage is satisfied before the closing, please notify our Law Department.

rc   Title No. 7099999

Restrictive covenants, conditions, easements, or leases of record, if any, are set forth below.

COVENANTS AND RESTRICTIONS in deed, Able Properties, Inc. to Roger Realtor, dated 9/15/27, recorded 9/16/27 in Liber 2111 cp. 333.

AND the party of the second part covenants and agrees that, he will not erect or cause or suffer to be erected on the above described premises, any building, other than a private dwelling and a private garage used in conjunction with a private dwelling, that is less than two stories in height, nor for any purpose other than first class residential. These covenants to be real convenants running with the land.

Title No. 7099999

MUNICIPAL DEPARTMENT VIOLATIONS

No state or municipal department searches for notices of violation of laws, regulations and ordinances filed therein are made UNLESS SPECIFICALLY REQUESTED BY THE APPLICANT. Such searches, if requested, are made by the particular municipal department and are called "Record Search" and disclose only those violations reported by the last inspection made by the City and do not show the present condition, which can be ascertained only by the applicant's requesting the City to make a new inspection and paying its fees therefore. Such searches are not continued to date of closing nor are new searches made even in event of adjournment or closing. ALL SEARCHES SPECIFICALLY REQUESTED ARE CHARGED FOR ADDITIONALLY AT COST TO THIS COMPANY PLUS THE APPLICABLE "SERVICE CHARGE."

This Company does not, in any event, insure that the buildings or other erections upon the premises or therein to comply with Federal, State and Municipal laws, regulations and ordinances, and therefore we assume no liability whatsoever by reason of the ordering of such searches and we do not insure their accuracy. We now set forth such information as has been furnished to us by the various departments:

Search made by Dept. of Buildings: REPORT DATED NOVEMBER 10, 1977
SHOWS NO VIOLATIONS

Search made by Fire Department: REPORT DATED NOVEMBER 10, 1977
SHOWS NO VIOLATIONS

Search made by　　　　　　　　Department:

CENTRAL VIOLATIONS BUREAU

We are advised by the Department of Buildings of the City of New York that since about July 1, 1961 our Fire Department, the Department of Health, the Department of Air Pollution and the Department of Water Supply, Gas and Electricity have been reporting violations issued by them affecting multiple dwellings and the Central Violations Bureau established pursuant to Section 328 of the Multiple Dwelling Law. In its report of its search for violations the Department of Buildings includes such violations affecting multiple dwellings files and the aforesaid departments in the central bureau.

STREET VAULTS

In NEW YORK CITY, if there is a STREET VAULT, it is suggested that the applicant investigate possible unpaid license fees and annual vault charges by the City of New York for the use of such vault, because the right to maintain the same IS NOT INSURED.

(SEE REVERSE SIDE FOR SPECIAL NOTICE RELATING TO STREET VAULTS)

SPECIAL NOTICE RELATING TO STREET VAULTS
(July 1, 1973)

A street vault is any subsurface opening, structure, or erection, whether or not covered over, to the extent that it extends from the building line under the street. If there is a street vault used in connection with the premises herein described, the applicant should acquaint himself with the provisions of Title Z of Chapter 46 of the Administrative Code of the City of New York which imposes an annual charge for maintaining such vaults in New York City.

Effective June 5, 1973, the Administrative Code of the City of New York was amended to provide that the annual vault charge imposed by this title shall become a lien, binding upon the premises immediately adjoining such vault on the date such charge is required to be paid (June 15) until the same is paid in full.

The person responsible for filing the return and paying the tax is the owner of the premises immediately adjoining the vault. A return must be filed with the Finance Administrator annually on Form A.V.C. which is available at the Office of the Bureau of City Collections. It must be filed and the charge paid by the 15th of June of each year, for the taxable period from June 1 through the following May 31. The return must be signed by the person required to file the same or by his duly authorized agent.

The charge is calculated according to the area of the vault. As to vaults no more than twelve feet in depth, the annual charge is one dollar a square foot of plane or surface area, with a minimum charge of five dollars. If a vault is more than twelve feet in depth, there is an additional charge.

The basic provisions for licensing vaults can be found in Section 692e-1.0 and the following sections of the Administrative Code (formerly Section 82d5-1.0). A vault may not be maintained in New York City unless a license is issued and a fee paid at the rate of not less than thirty cents nor more than two dollars a square foot. The license is revocable without compensation at the will of the city if the space is needed for a public purpose.

Returns must be filed with the Office of Special Taxes of the Finance Adminstration, 139 Centre Street, New York, N.Y. 10013, on or before the due date thereof. Payment of the annual vault charge may be made in cash, check or money order drawn to the order of the City Collector. Checks or money orders should be sent with the return to the Office of Special Taxes. Cash payments must be made only to the cashiers designated for that purpose at the borough offices of the Bureau of City Collections and must be presented with the return before 3:00 o'clock, P.M., Monday through Friday. Under no circumstances should cash be sent by mail. If the person required to pay the annual vault charge mails his return, it should be posted in ample time so as to reach the Office of Special Taxes on or before the due date.

Any person failing to file a return or to pay over any annual vault charge to the Finance Administrator within the time required by law shall be subject to a penalty of five percent of the amount due, plus interest at the rate of one percent of such vault charge for each month of delay excepting the first month after such return was required to be filed or such vault charge became due.

The title policy does not insure the right to maintain street vaults.

If closed by examining counsel the communication on the reverse side hereof must also be completed and signed by said examining counsel.

Title No. 7099999

REPORT OF CLOSING

By whom closed_____ Date Closed_____

Transaction closed at office of _____

The persons present were:

Name	Address	Interest

The identity of the persons executing the papers delivered on closing was established by the following evidence:

_____

Title policy is to be sent

(Fee)—To_____

Address _____

Fee ☐ Mtge. ☐ policy delivered on closing

(Mtge.)—To _____

Address _____

The following instruments were executed and delivered:

1. Kind of instrument_____

   By_____

   _____

   To or With_____

   _____

   _____

   Dated_____ Recorded_____

   L._____p.____ Trust Clause?____

   Consideration or amount $_____

2. Kind of instrument_____

   By_____

   To or With_____

   _____

   _____

   Dated_____ Recorded_____

   L._____p.____ Trust Clause?____

   Consideration or amount $_____

CLOSER: (a) Always PRINT Name of Insured fully and completely and write all other names legibly. (b) when there are two persons, indicate whether husband or wife. (c) if first names are unusual indicate whether male or female. Abstract fully terms of payment of any mortgage delivered on closing. Show addresses of all grantees and individual mortgagees.

Other information and recitals

Stamps affixed $ _____

_____

_____

_____

_____

Stamps affixed $ _____

_____

_____

_____

_____

_____

_____

REPORT OF CLOSING (Cont'd)

3. Kind of instrument _____

   By_____

   _____

   To or With_____

   _____

   Dated_____ Recorded_____

   L.____p.____ Trust Clause?_____

   Consideration or amount $_____

   Other information and recitals

   Stamps affixed $ _____

   _____

   _____

   _____

   _____

   _____

   _____

   _____

4. Kind of instrument_____

   By_____

   _____

   To or With_____

   _____

   Dated_____ Recorded_____

   L.____p.____ Trust Clause?_____

   Consideration or amount $_____

   Stamps affixed $ _____

   _____

   _____

   _____

   _____

   _____

   _____

   _____

FOR EXAMINING COUNSEL'S USE IN PAYING COMPANY'S CHARGES	FOR CASHIER'S USE
Insurance Charges . . . . $ __	
U.S. Court, Superior Court and Tax Searches $ __	Received $^{CASH}_{CHECK}$ for
Revenue Stamps . . . . $ __	$_____
Recording . . . . $ __	on _____, 19____
$ __	
Total $ ___	(Cashier)

The undersigned certifies that all searches have been duly continued from the date of the Certificate of Title furnished by the undersigned to _____ at   M. and that any returns found on such continuation have been adequately reflected in said Certificate of Title. The closing instruments numbering _____ have been abstracted above. No other instruments were delivered on closing.

_____

Examining Counsel

Bargain-and-sale deeds do not contain any of the warranty covenants just mentioned, but the seller does convey title absolutely. In some states, the seller will also agree to covenant in a bargain-and-sale deed that he or she has not encumbered the property in any way. The seller, however, has no responsibility to the buyer for acts of previous owners.

Quitclaim deeds contain no warranties or covenants at all. The seller is merely releasing any interest he or she may have in the title to the property. Quitclaim deeds are often used to correct title defects that may appear in the public record. The buyer agrees to be liable for any liens or encumbrances and has no right to recover any losses sustained from the deed transferred by the seller.

TYPES OF OWNERSHIP

When you are buying a house, ask your attorney about the form in which you should take title. There are four basic choices, and it is advantageous to review your income, assets, investment outlook, and personal feeling in some detail before choosing. The wrong choice can result in paying additional taxes or other inconveniences. The basic types of ownership are:

1. *In a husband's or wife's name only.*
2. *Tenancy in common* is ownership of property by two or more persons with an interest that may be equal or unequal. Generally, there is unity of possession but no right of *survivorship*—that is, upon the death of one of the owners, his or her interest goes to heirs through a will and not to the other owner(s). This is exactly the opposite of joint tenancy or tenancy by the entirety.
3. In *joint tenancy*, the owners have a right of survivorship, which means that upon death, the other owners receive the interest of the deceased owner. The joint tenants must also have an equal fractional interest in the property. Joint tenants may sell or give away their interest during life. When this happens, it destroys the joint tenancy, and the owners become tenants in common.
4. *Tenants by the entirety* is similar to joint tenancy but exists between a husband and wife. It is based on the concept that husband and wife are one. Upon the death of either spouse, his or her interest is transferred to the surviving spouse. Unlike joint tenancy, however, a spouse may not transfer interest in the property without the consent of the other spouse. A divorce converts tenants by the entirety to tenants in common. Tenants by the entirety is not recognized in all areas of the United States.

Lawyers favor tenants in common because it avoids the survivorship problem of automatically passing interest in property upon death to the other joint tenant. For married persons, a joint-tenant purchase of a house denies either spouse the right to give away their interest through a will. Only if the property is given away prior to death will the half-interest not pass automatically upon death to the surviving tenant. Joint tenancy may also present the problem of one spouse having to pay a gift tax or inheritance tax when the other spouse dies.

Still, joint tenancy is a popular way of taking title to a home. Psychologically, it gives each spouse the security of owning part of what is usually their largest single asset. Only you, your spouse, and your attorney can decide what is best for you after reviewing your particular situation.

SURVEY

A survey is a detailed pictorial description of a property and shows its exact dimensions. It should show the location of all structures, walls, and easements that affect the land. (See Fig. 6.1.) The normal fee for a survey varies throughout

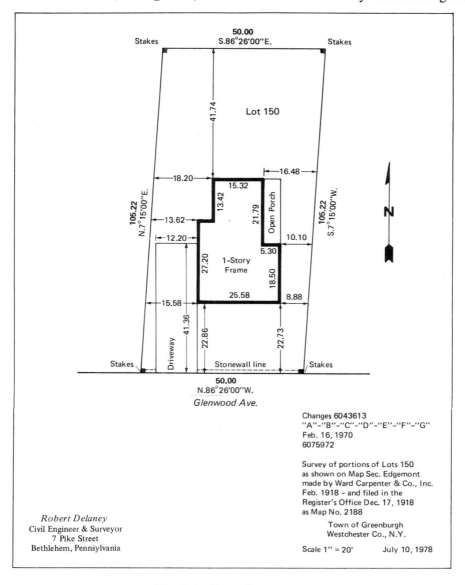

Fig. 6.1. Sample survey

the country, but is generally in the range of $75 to $250. Most lending institutions will want a survey before they issue a mortgage. The buyer may be able to save this expense by asking for the seller's survey. If the seller can locate it and if the property has not changed substantially, the lender may accept the old survey. It is worth a try.

CONTRACT OF SALE

The *Contract of Sale* fixes the terms agreed upon between the buyer and the seller. It specifies a description of the property sufficient to identify it, selling price, terms of payment, and names and addresses of seller and buyer. Such instruments vary, not only because of the different purposes of the seller and buyer, but also because of differences among state, county, and municipal laws. This is another good reason to choose a local attorney who is aware of the laws and customs in the area where you wish to buy.

The attorney will want to specify within the Contract of Sale any personal property included in the transaction. In addition, it is likely that the contract will condition itself on several crucial events. One of the most common conditions is the buyer's obtaining a commitment letter from a lending institution. This assures the buyer of mortgage funds above the down payment to pay the seller's full price. Other things frequently put in the Contract of Sale are:

1. *Termite clause*, which gives the purchaser a specific period of time to have a termite inspection of the house. If there is damage and it exceeds a certain cost, the seller may elect to correct the condition or cancel the contract.
2. *Vacant delivery* specifies that the seller agrees to deliver the premises vacant on the date of closing.
3. *Seller representations*. The seller represents that plumbing, heating and electrical systems will be in working order at the time of closing.
4. *Down-payment escrow*. Whenever possible, the seller or the attorney should hold the down payment in escrow pending obtaining a commitment letter or even until the closing.
5. *Date, time, and place* for closing of title should be specified. At that time, the seller will be paid, and the buyer will receive a deed to the property. Closing is also called *settlement* because all expenses of transfer are paid at that time.

The customary down payment given at the Contract of Sale is 10% of the purchase price, which can be adjusted depending on the desires of the buyer and seller. The buyer can also negotiate with the seller about who pays various settlement fees and other charges, and put it in the contract. Otherwise, much of the language in a Contract of Sale can be found on a standard, printed contract form. You should read the Contract of Sale, and ask your attorney to explain any language that is not clear.

7. Securing a Mortgage

SELECTING A LENDER

If you are purchasing a new development house, the first place to look for financing is to the developer. Many times, a sponsor will use attractive financing with low down payments to aid in the sale of the houses. If you are buying a house from an individual seller, see if the mortgage is assignable and whether its terms are attractive compared to those available from regular mortgage sources. Finally, see if the seller can extend a purchase-money mortgage for part of the purchase price. (In a purchase-money mortgage, the seller lends part of the price in the same way regular mortgage sources do.) If none of these options are available, then you will have to seek a loan from a financial institution.

All lenders are not alike. The price of settlement services, which will be discussed in detail in this chapter, can vary greatly. In any case, the federal Real Estate Settlement Procedures Act (RESPA) will help protect you. When you submit a written application for a loan, the lender is required to give you a booklet on settlement costs. In addition, the lender must give you a good-faith estimate for each settlement charge that he or she anticipates you will pay. Since charges vary by locality, this service is extremely helpful.

You may also want to request a truth-in-lending statement when you apply for a mortgage loan. This will disclose the annual percentage rate you will pay on the outstanding balance. The annual percentage rate may be higher than the contract rate in your mortgage because it includes discount points, financing charges, and certain other fees that the lender requires.

You should use Worksheet 5 to compile loan information and to list settlement charges that you will have to pay to different lending institutions. The following items will enable you to complete the worksheet. Remember, this is a complete listing, and it is unlikely that a single lender will require more than a few of these fees.

800. *Items payable in connection with loan* are the fees that lenders charge to process, approve, and make a mortgage loan.

801. *Loan origination fee* covers the lender's administrative costs in processing the loan. Often expressed as a percentage of the loan, the fee will vary among lenders and from locality to locality. Generally, the buyer pays the fee unless another arrangement has been made with the seller and written into the sales contract.

802. *Loan discount,* often called *points,* is a one-time charge used to adjust the yield on the loan to what the market conditions demand. It is used to offset constraints placed on interest rates by state or federal regulations. Each point is equal to 1% of the mortgage amount. For example, if a lender charges three points on a $30,000 loan, the total charge is $900.

803. *Appraisal fee* pays for a statement of property value for the lender, which is made by an independent appraiser or by a member of the lender's staff. This charge may vary significantly from transaction to transaction. The lender needs to know if the value of the property is sufficient to secure the loan should the buyer fail to repay it according to the provisions of the mortgage contract, thus forcing the lender to foreclose and take title to the house and property.

In determining the value, the appraiser inspects the home and the neighborhood, and considers sale prices of comparable houses as well as other factors. The appraisal report may contain photographs and other valuable information. It will provide the factual data upon which the appraiser based the appraised value. Ask the lender for a copy of the appraisal report, or review the original.

WORKSHEET 5
SETTLEMENT COSTS

			Lender 1	Lender 2	Lender 3
800. ITEMS PAYABLE IN CONNECTION WITH LOAN					
801.	Loan Origination Fee	%			
802.	Loan Discount	%			
803.	Appraisal Fee				
804.	Credit Report				
805.	Lender's Inspection Fee				
806.	Mortgage Insurance Application Fee to				
807.	Assumption Fee				
808.					
809.					
810.					
811.					
900. ITEMS REQUIRED BY LENDER TO BE PAID IN ADVANCE					
901.	Interest from to @ $ /day				
902.	Mortgage Insurance Premium for months				
903.	Hazard Insurance Premium for years				
904.	years				
905.					
1000. RESERVES DEPOSITED WITH LENDER					
1001.	Hazard insurance	months @ $ per month			
1002.	Mortgage insurance	months @ $ per month			
1003.	City property taxes	months @ $ per month			
1004.	County property taxes	months @ $ per month			
1005.	Annual assessments	months @ $ per month			
1006.		months @ $ per month			
1007.		months @ $ per month			
1008.		months @ $ per month			
1100. TITLE CHARGES					
1101.	Settlement or closing fee				
1102.	Abstract or title search				
1103.	Title examination				
1104.	Title insurance binder				
1105.	Document preparation				
1106.	Notary fees				
1107.	Attorney's fees				
	(includes above items numbers;				
1108.	Title insurance				
	(includes above items numbers;				
1109.	Lender's coverage $				
1110.	Owner's coverage $				
1111.					
1112.					
1113.					
1200. GOVERNMENT RECORDING AND TRANSFER CHARGES					
1201.	Recording fees: Deed $; Mortgage $; Releases $				
1202.	City/county tax/stamps: Deed $; Mortgage $				
1203.	State tax/stamps: Deed $; Mortgage $				
1204.					
1205.					
1300. ADDITIONAL SETTLEMENT CHARGES					
1301.	Survey				
1302.	Pest inspection				
1303.					
1304.					
1305.					
1400.	**TOTAL SETTLEMENT CHARGES**				

804. *Credit report fee* covers the cost of the credit report, which shows how the buyer has handled other credit transactions. The lender uses this report—in conjunction with information the buyer submitted with the application regarding income, outstanding bills, and employment—to determine (1) whether the buyer is an acceptable credit risk and (2) how much money to lend the buyer.

805. *Lender's inspection fee* covers inspections, often on newly constructed housing, made by personnel of the lending institution or an outside inspector. The quality and suitability of construction is important if the lender must foreclose, take title, and resell the property.

806. *Mortgage insurance application fee* covers processing the application for private mortgage insurance, which may be required on certain loans. It may cover both the appraisal and application fee.

807. *Assumption fee* is charged for processing papers for cases in which the buyer takes over payments on the prior loan of the seller.

900. *Items required by lender to be paid in advance* include such items as interest, mortgage insurance premium, and hazard insurance premium that the buyer may be required to prepay at the time of settlement. Prepayment gives the lender assurance that adequate insurance is in effect.

901. *Interest* accrues on the mortgage from the date of settlement to the beginning of the period covered by the first monthly payment. Lenders usually require that borrowers pay the interest at settlement. For example, suppose the settlement takes place on May 17, and the first regular monthly payment, to cover interest charges for the month of June, is due June 12. On the settlement date, the lender will collect the interest for the period from May 17 to June 12. So, if the amount borrowed is $40,000 at 9% interest, the interest item would be $256.44. (This amount would be entered on Worksheet 5, line 901.)

902. *Mortgage insurance* protects the lender from loss due to payment default by the owner. The lender may require the buyer to pay the first premium in advance, on the day of settlement. The premium may cover a specific number of months or a year in advance. With this insurance protection, the lender is willing to make a larger loan, thus reducing the down-payment requirements. This type of insurance should not be confused with mortgage life, credit life, or disability insurance designed to pay off a mortgage in the event of physical disability or death of the borrower.

903. *Hazard insurance* protects the buyer and the lender against losses due to fire, windstorm, and natural hazards. This coverage may be included in a homeowners policy, which insures against additional risks such as personal liability and thrift. Lenders often require payment of the first year's premium at settlement.

1000. *Reserves deposited with lenders* (sometimes called *escrow* or *impound* accounts) are funds held in an account by the lender to insure future payment for such recurring items as real-estate taxes and other insurance.

Buyers usually have to pay an initial amount for each of these items to start the reserve account at the time of settlement. A portion of the regular monthly mortgage payments required by the lender is added to the reserve account.

Thus, when the recurring expense becomes due, the buyer will have saved sufficient funds to pay for it.

1001. *Hazard insurance.* The lender determines the amount of money that must be placed in the reserve in order to pay the next insurance premium when due.

1002. *Mortgage insurance.* Mortgage insurance pays off the remaining balance of the mortgage obligation if the buyer should die. The lender may require that part of the total annual premium be placed in the reserve account at settlement.

1003/1004. *City/county property taxes.* The lender may require a regular monthly payment to the reserve account for property taxes. This payment is added to the monthly mortgage payment amount and raises the total paid each month. However, the lender does not keep the additional portion. Instead, it is escrowed and paid to the appropriate tax authority when property taxes fall due.

1005. *Annual assessments* is a reserve item covering assessments that may be imposed by subdivisions or municipalities for special improvements (such as sidewalks, sewers, or paving) or fees.

OTHER CLOSING COSTS

The settlement fees and services required by a particular lender are not the only expenses paid at closing. In addition to the closing costs just listed, there may be the following:

1. *Survey fee* for a professional survey to determine (1) the exact location of the house on the property and (2) whether others have easements or rights-of-way on the property.

2. *Termite or pest inspection* determines if there has been any damage to the property that should be corrected. Although some lenders require such an inspection, generally it is the buyer who insists on the right to inspect for insect or pest damage.

3. *Mortgage taxes* are required by some state and local authorities at the time a new mortgage is issued by a lending institution. The amount can be quite substantial.

4. *Adjustments* are usually made between the buyer and seller for property or other taxes that are paid annually or semiannually. This process, called *proration,* will be discussed in detail in the next chapter.

5. *Personal property* such as rugs, draperies, washing machines, and built-in shelving not included in the sales price are paid for by the purchaser.

COMMITMENT LETTERS

Most Contracts of Sale are conditioned on the buyer's ability to obtain a mortgage. They specify a period of time in which the purchaser must find a lending institution willing to extend a mortgage for a particular term of years, at a specific interest rate, and in a certain dollar amount. Purchasers unable to obtain the

EXHIBIT 7.1

SAMPLE COMMITMENT
LETTER
AND DISCLOSURE
STATEMENT

December 14, 1978

Arthur M. and Marcia H. Sloan
27 Stebbins Ave.
Chicago, Illinois 11111

Re: 18 Justin Way
Cherry Hill
Chicago County
Chicago

Dear Applicants:

Our Real Estate Committee has approved the mortgage application submitted on the captioned premises of $50,000 for 30 years self-liquidating with interest at the rate of 8½%. All payments shall be made monthly including 1/12th of the real estate taxes and 1/12th of the insurance premiums. This commitment is subject to a verification of the information furnished to us in your preliminary application.

The loan is to be secured by Bond or Note of Arthur M. and Marcia H. Sloan.

Title (Deed) will be in the name of Arthur N. and Marcia H. Sloan.

The undersigned agrees that final approval and closing is contingent upon the following:

Loan is to close on or before April 9th, 1979.

Examination and approval of title by attorneys for Bank, and the preparation of all instruments by said attorneys on forms customarily used by the Bank in similar transactions.

Delivery of Certificate of Occupancy for use specified.

Delivery of hazard insurance and other insurance if required, in such companies and amounts and written in such manner as shall be satisfactory to the bank.

Verification and approval by the Bank of the borrower's credit.

It is a condition that no secondary financing in addition to the First Mortgage herein has been or is being placed on this property in connection with the sale or refinancing of the property.

Delivery of Flood Hazard Insurance is required by Regulation H of the Federal Reserve Board if the property is in a flood hazard area. You will be required to pay the necessary closing charges and expenses in connection with the loan.

Documents must be satisfactory in form and substance to our attorney.

Fire Insurance policy for at least $50,000

Flood insurance not required. Closing fee of $75.00 to be paid to closing attorney, by the mortgagor, at the time of closing.

If the Bank is requested to use an existing completion survey, unless one has already been furnished, a copy must be furnished to us within 10 days of date.

The applicant understands that loan documents will contain an acceleration clause, giving the mortgagee the right at its option to accelerate the unpaid balance of principal of the loan in the event the property is sold.

Very truly yours,
THE FIRST SAVINGS BANK

Robert T. Doe
Assistant Vice President

Kindly indicate your acceptance of this commitment by signing and returning the copy of this letter on or before December 28th, 1978 together with the receipted copy of the disclosure statement.

Approved and accepted
this   day of   , 19

_____
Arthur Mace Sloan

_____
Marcia Harriet Sloan

EXHIBIT 7.1 (Continued)

DISCLOSURE STATEMENT
CONVENTIONAL FIRST MORTGATE LOAN TO FINANCE
PURCHASE OF DWELLING

DATE   December 15th, 1977

BORROWER'S NAME AND ADDRESS Arthur M. and Marcia H. Sloan
LENDER: THE FIRST SAVINGS BANK, 12 Southway, Chicago, Illinois 11111
AMOUNT OF LOAN: $50,000.
TERM: 30 YRS.
INTEREST RATE: 8½% PER ANNUM
360 SUCCEEDING MONTHLY INSTALLMENTS OF PRINCIPAL AND INTEREST. EACH IN THE AMOUNT OF $384.45

An additional installment of interest only shall be due if the interest from the date of the bond to the date of the first payment is less than a month.

With each monthly installment of principal and interest, there will be due an additional sum, for the mortgagors escrow account, equivalent to 1/12 of the following

□ANNUAL TAXES   □ANNUAL FIRE AND EXTENDED
                                            COVERAGE INSURANCE

Fire insurance required may be obtained through your own broker or agent provided the insurance company is acceptable to the Bank. Such insurance may not be purchased from this Bank.

PREPAID FINANCE CHARGES: DISBURSEMENTS:

Service Charge	$_____	Recording Fees:
Origination Fee	$_____	Mortgage Tax _____
Loan Fee Paid By:		Mortgage Recording Fee: $14.00 Est.
Seller:	$_____	
Broker:	$_____	
	$_____	
Total Prepaid FINANCE CHARGE	$____None____	

Amount Financed $50,000.   ANNUAL PERCENTAGE RATE 8½%

The security interest for this loan transaction will be a first mortgage lien on premises:

18	Justin Way	Chicago	Cherry County	Illinois	75 × 100
(NO.)	(STREET)	(CITY)	(COUNTY)	(STATE)	(PLOT SIZE)

more particularly to be described in the mortgage with a certified description from the insuring title company, a copy of which will be furnished to you as promptly as practicable.

The loan documents will include the following provisions—

Late Payment Provision: "In the event that any payment due hereunder shall become overdue for a period in excess of fifteen (15) days, a late charge of two (2¢) cents for each dollar ($1.00) so overdue shall be charged by the holder hereof for the purpose of defraying the expense incipient to handling such delinquent payment, which obligors agree to pay."

Prepayment Provision: "AND IT IS FURTHER EXPRESSLY AGREED that on or after one year from the date hereof, the obligor shall have the right to prepay the unpaid principal balance owing on this loan, in whole or in part, without penalty, together with interest thereon to the date of payment."

After Acquired Property Provision: "TOGETHER WITH all attachments, appliances, fittings, furnishings, fixtures and articles of personal property, and each and every improvement, now in or upon or which shall hereafter be placed in or upon the above described premises, adapted to and/or necessary for the proper use and enjoyment of the same, all of which are hereby represented and declared by the mortgagor to be the sold and unconditional property of the mortgagor and to be part of the freehold and covered by this mortgage, and subject to the same laws and limitations applicable to real property. If the lien of this mortgage be subject to a conditional bill of sale or chattle mortgage covering any such property, then in the event of any default in this mortgage all the right, title and interst of the mortgagor, in and to any and all such personal property is hereby assigned to the mortgagee, together with the benefits of any deposits or payments now or hereafter made thereon by the mortgagor or the predecessors or successors in title to the mortgagor in the mortgaged premises.''

Receipt of a copy of this statement on_____ is hereby acknowledged.

_____
Arthur M. Sloan

B&M 194 (REV. 9/74)   REAL ESTATE DEPARTMENT _____
Marcia Harriet Sloan

requisite mortgage have the right to cancel the contract. The lending institution that received the mortgage application will check up on the credit, employment, and assets of the purchaser and will usually appraise the property. When the lender is satisfied that the loan is worthwhile, a commitment letter is issued to the purchaser for a specific mortgage. This completes the condition and assures the parties that a sale will take place according to the terms of the Contract of Sale. (See Exhibit 7.1.)

8. Getting Through the Closing

PRORATION

Proration is the division of the various obligations running with the property between the buyer and seller at closing. In general, these will be real-estate taxes for the current year, school taxes for the current year, interest on a mortgage assumed by the buyer, water bills, electricity bills, heating oil remaining in the oil tank, and prepaid insurance premiums.

For real-estate taxes and school taxes, the process is somewhat involved. In many areas, school taxes are paid twice each year but real-estate taxes only once each year. Additionally, the month in which such taxes are due may not coincide with the calendar year. For example, real-estate taxes of $1200 may be due on January 1, and total school taxes of $1080 may be due in $540 installments on March 1 and September 1. (See Fig. 8.1.) If a closing is on June 15, it will be necessary to divide the responsibility for these taxes between the seller and purchaser. The seller had to pay a full 12 months of real-estate taxes ($1200) on January 1. As of the closing, he will have lived there five and a half months and will be entitled to a refund of six and a half months of real-estate taxes. Since the monthly cost is $100, the buyer will reimburse the seller $650. School taxes for six months were paid on March 1 in the amount of $540 ($90 per month). Since the seller will have lived in the house three and a half months since then, he will be reimbursed by the buyer in the amount of $225 for school taxes.

Real-Estate Taxes		School Taxes			Date of Closing		School Taxes				
					15						
Jan.	Feb.	Mar.	Apr.	May	June	July	Aug.	Sept.	Oct.	Nov.	Dec.

Fig. 8.1

Interest and utility bills are usually divided using information from the bank and the utility company. The buyer's lawyer will check to be certain that all financial responsibilities of the seller that might pass to the buyer are paid in full. If the house has a large tank of oil, the oil is measured and multiplied by the current price per gallon. If there is a large tank (e.g., 1000 gallons) and it is almost full, a substantial cash outlay may be required at closing.

You should get a good idea of the total of these charges before the actual closing. Ask your attorney to furnish a detailed breakdown of anticipated expenses so that everything goes smoothly.

AGENDA FOR CLOSING

As mentioned earlier, closing is the time when the buyer and seller are ready to complete transfer of the deed to the property. All of the terms of the Contract of Sale must be carried out. If there is an existing mortgage owed by the seller to a lending institution, and it will not be assumed by the buyer, it must be paid off at closing. Once the old mortgage is satisfied during the closing, the new lender will extend a mortgage as outlined in the commitment letter. Usually, the lender will divide the amount of the mortgage funds into two checks. One is given to the previous lending institution to pay off the old mortgage; the balance goes to the seller. The following agenda is common:

1. The title search and survey are examined to clear up any objections or problems.
2. Taxes and other charges are divided.
3. The deed is examined to be certain it accurately describes the premises.

4. Proof of adequate fire insurance is presented.
5. The brokerage fee for sale of the premises is paid.
6. A new bond and mortgage are issued to the purchaser.
7. The old mortgage is paid, and a certificate of satisfaction is issued.
8. The balance of the funds are given to the seller as his or her equity in the property.
9. If it is a new house, inspection and occupancy certificates are given to the buyer.
10. Recording fees are paid.
11. The deed is signed over to the buyer.
12. Keys to the premises are given to the buyer by the seller.

Most closings are attended by the seller(s), attorney of seller(s), lending institution of seller(s), purchaser(s), attorney of purchaser(s), lending institution of purchaser(s), title insurance company, and broker. Don't hesitate to ask questions or take the time to read documents before you sign them. Expect to write many checks.

UNIFORM SETTLEMENT STATEMENT

Exhibit 8.1 is an example of a Uniform Settlement Statement, which is provided to the buyer at the closing. Observe that Sections A through I contain information about the loan and the parties involved in the settlement. Sections J and K summarize all monies that are adjusted between the purchaser, who is called the *borrower,* and the seller. Section L has a part on broker's commission and on the information gathered in Worksheet 5 on settlement services required by the lending institution you have chosen.

RECORDING

Recording of a deed means that a local recording clerk files the deed in the proper index to give notice of ownership to the general public. It is an important part of guaranteeing that ownership is absolute. In some areas, the failure to record a deed can have a disastrous result for a buyer. A dishonest seller could sell the same house to an innocent second purchaser who would not have notice of the previous purchase because of the unrecorded deed. If the second purchaser records first, he or she may be declared the owner.

ESCROW CLOSINGS

In some parts of the United States, there is no actual meeting for a closing. Instead, an escrow agent (such as a lender, title company, attorney, or escrow

EXHIBIT 8.1

HUD-1 REV. 5/76

FORM APPROVED OMB NO. 63-R-1501

A.		B. TYPE OF LOAN

U.S. DEPARTMENT OF HOUSING AND URBAN DEVELOPMENT

SETTLEMENT STATEMENT

1. ☐ FHA   2. ☐ FMHA   3. ☐ CONV. UNINS.
4. ☐ VA   5. ☐ CONV. INS.

6. FILE NUMBER:	7. LOAN NUMBER:

8. MORTGAGE INSURANCE CASE NUMBER:

X 88 p. 1, Julius Blumberg, Inc., NYC 10013

C. **NOTE:** This form is furnished to give you a statement of actual settlement costs. Amounts paid to and by the settlement agent are shown. Items marked "(p.o.c.)" were paid outside the closing; they are shown here for informational purposes and are not included in totals.

D. NAME OF BORROWER:	E. NAME OF SELLER:	F. NAME OF LENDER:

G. PROPERTY LOCATION:	H. SETTLEMENT AGENT:	PLACE OF SETTLEMENT
	I. SETTLEMENT DATE:	

J. SUMMARY OF BORROWER'S TRANSACTION		K. SUMMARY OF SELLER'S TRANSACTION	
100. **GROSS AMOUNT DUE FROM BORROWER:**		400. **GROSS AMOUNT DUE TO SELLER:**	
101. Contract sales price		401. Contract sales price	
102. Personal property		402. Personal property	
103. Settlement charges to borrower (line 1400)		403.	
104.		404.	
105.		405.	
Adjustments for items paid by seller in advance		*Adjustments for items paid by seller in advance*	
106. City/town taxes to		406. City/town taxes to	
107. County taxes to		407. County taxes to	
108. Assessments to		408. Assessments to	
109.		409.	
110.		410.	
111.		411.	
112.		412.	
120. **GROSS AMOUNT DUE FROM BORROWER**		420. **GROSS AMOUNT DUE TO SELLER**	
200. **AMOUNTS PAID BY OR IN BEHALF OF BORROWER:**		500. **REDUCTIONS IN AMOUNT DUE TO SELLER:**	
201. Deposit or earnest money		501. Excess deposit (see instructions)	
202. Principal amount of new loan(s)		502. Settlement charges to seller (line 1400)	
203. Existing loan(s) taken subject to		503. Existing loan(s) taken subject to	
204.		504. Payoff of first mortgage loan	
205.		505. Payoff of second mortgage loan	
206.		506.	
207.		507.	
208.		508.	
209.		509.	
Adjustments for items unpaid by seller:		*Adjustments for items unpaid by seller:*	
210. City/town taxes to		510. City/town taxes to	
211. County taxes to		511. County taxes to	
212. Assessments to		512. Assessments to	
213.		513.	
214.		514.	
215.		515.	
216.		516.	
217.		517.	
218.		518.	
219.		519.	
220. **TOTAL PAID BY/FOR BORROWER**		520. **TOTAL REDUCTION AMOUNT DUE SELLER**	
300. **CASH AT SETTLEMENT FROM/TO BORROWER**		600. **CASH AT SETTLEMENT TO/FROM SELLER**	
301. Gross amount due from borrower (line 120)		601. Gross amount due to seller (line 420)	
302. Less amounts paid by/for borrower (line 220)	( )	602. Less reductions in amt. due to seller (line 520)	( )
303. **CASH (☐ FROM) (☐ TO) BORROWER**		603. **CASH (☐ TO) (☐ FROM) SELLER**	

EXHIBIT 8.1 *(Continued)*

L. SETTLEMENT CHARGES

	PAID FROM BORROWER'S FUNDS AT SETTLEMENT	PAID FROM SELLER'S FUNDS AT SETTLEMENT
700. TOTAL SALES/BROKER'S COMMISSION based on price $ @ % =		
Division of Commission (line 700) as follows:		
701. $ to		
702. $ to		
703. Commission paid at Settlement		
704.		
800. ITEMS PAYABLE IN CONNECTION WITH LOAN		
801. Loan Origination Fee %		
802. Loan Discount %		
803. Appraisal Fee to		
804. Credit Report to		
805. Lender's Inspection Fee		
806. Mortgage Insurance Application Fee to		
807. Assumption Fee		
808.		
809.		
810.		
811.		
900. ITEMS REQUIRED BY LENDER TO BE PAID IN ADVANCE		
901. Interest from to @ $ /day		
902. Mortgage Insurance Premium for months to		
903. Hazard Insurance Premium for years to		
904. years to		
905.		
1000. RESERVES DEPOSITED WITH LENDER		
1001. Hazard insurance months @ $ per month		
1002. Mortgage insurance months @ $ per month		
1003. City property taxes months @ $ per month		
1004. County property taxes months @ $ per month		
1005. Annual assessments months @ $ per month		
1006. months @ $ per month		
1007. months @ $ per month		
1008. months @ $ per month		
1100. TITLE CHARGES		
1101. Settlement or closing fee to		
1102. Abstract or title search to		
1103. Title examination to		
1104. Title insurance binder to		
1105. Document preparation to		
1106. Notary fees to		
1107. Attorney's fees to		
(includes above items numbers; *)*		
1108. Title insurance to		
(includes above items numbers; *)*		
1109. Lender's coverage $		
1110. Owner's coverage $		
1111.		
1112.		
1113.		
1200. GOVERNMENT RECORDING AND TRANSFER CHARGES		
1201. Recording fees: Deed $; Mortgage $; Releases $		
1202. City/county tax/stamps: Deed $; Mortgage $		
1203. State tax/stamps: Deed $; Mortgage $		
1204.		
1205.		
1300. ADDITIONAL SETTLEMENT CHARGES		
1301. Survey to		
1302. Pest inspection to		
1303.		
1304.		
1305.		
1400. **TOTAL SETTLEMENT CHARGES** *(enter on lines 103, Section J and 502, Section K)*		

We, the undersigned, identified as Borrower in section D hereof and Seller in section E hereof, hereby acknowledge receipt of this completed Uniform Settlement Statement (pages 1 & 2) on   19

Borrower: Seller:

_____   _____

_____   _____

company) completes the sale under the terms of an escrow agreement. The escrow agent requests title reports, drafts documents, pays off loans, acquires insurance, settles costs of services, and records the appropriate documents. When all papers and monies have been properly deposited and executed, the escrow is closed. In such cases, the escrow agent sends the Uniform Settlement Statement to the buyer by mail.

REPORT OF CLOSING

The attorney should furnish the buyer with a detailed report of all activities that went on during the closing of title. The buyer will probably forget some of the minor points of the closing since so many exchanges take place. This report is a valuable aid because it is a summary that can be referred to if problems develop after closing.

The title report shown in Exhibit 6.2 contained one example of a report of closing (see pp. 96–97), but your attorney may prefer another format. The following, however, should be included:

1. Parties present, and their affiliation and address
2. Time, date, and place of closing
3. Description of all checks including numbers, bank, amount, party to whom issued, party who issued, and endorsements if any
4. Brief description of instruments issued and delivered
5. All relevant events, such as the delivery of deed and keys to the buyer

9. After You Move In

Unless you can afford a custom-built house, it is unlikely that everything in your new home will be perfect when you move in. Even the most thorough prior inspection cannot discover the minor flaws that become apparent only after you have lived in a house. If you buy an older structure, be prepared to repair or modernize to some degree. If you expect to replace any major items over time, establish a savings account to fund such expenditures.

It is important to keep you house up to date and thus protect your investment. If a new kitchen is needed, plan it and build it. Not only will you enjoy the convenience, but the value of the house will stay within the market price of similar houses.

The following examples present 10 common situations that confront the house buyer. If you've read the first eight chapters carefully, you should be able to spot the potential pitfalls in each situation.

EXAMPLE 1

Jane and Rob were forced to move to another state because of a job transfer. Although unfamiliar with the new area, they decided to purchase a house immediately for the sake of their young son Eric. A new development just outside of town advertised very low priced houses with most of the features they wanted. Jane and Rob inspected the structure of the house completely and were satisfied with its quality. They could not understand why, with prices so reasonable, so many of the houses remained unsold. The following spring thaw gave them the answer. All of the development homes were built on lowlands, which flooded with the melting of winter snows. There was no local real-estate authority to prohibit an unscrupulous developer from constructing houses on this unsuitable property.

Conclusions: Always investigate the land under a house for natural and man-made problems

Ask neighbors about such problems as flooding, mudslides, or improper landfill.

Many unsold homes should make you extra cautious.

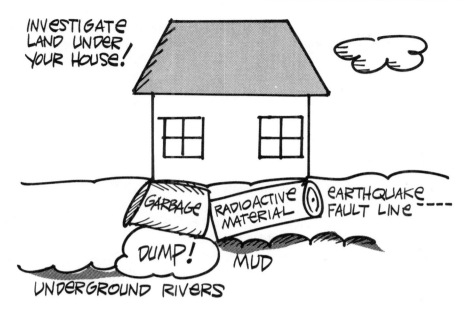

EXAMPLE 2

Kay and Jerry saw a model home that had everything they'd always wanted—beautiful carpeting, high-quality kitchen appliances, built-in hardwood shelves in several rooms, carved wooden doors, customized bathrooms, and a magnificent fireplace. The exterior had a slate roof with copper gutters and drainpipes. The agent said that the developer was only going to build 12 such homes and that only one more could be sold. Since the developer was providing financing, they were told they could save a legal fee for their own lawyer, and the bank's. Kay and Jerry had already saved the down payment, so they decided on the spot to buy. When the house was finally constructed, however, it had none of the luxury amenities shown in the model, and the kitchen appliances were strictly bottom of the line. In the meantime, the mortgage that Kay and Jerry signed had been sold to a local bank so they could not hold up their payments.

Conclusions: Know what you are buying, and have it specified in detail in the sales contract. Include model numbers and names for all kitchen appliances.

Never buy without consulting your own attorney.

EXAMPLE 3

One summer, Joanne, a suburban school teacher, decided to invest in a house that was under construction. The sales agent promised that it would be completed by late fall. However, nothing in the Contract of Sale guaranteed occupancy on a specific date. Nevertheless, in November, Joanne gave up her apartment so that she would not have to renew the lease. She put her furniture in storage and moved into a hotel. By April, the house was still not available for occupancy, yet Joanne risked losing her $4000 down payment if she tried to rescind the contract.

Conclusions: Don't depend on oral promises for a date of occupancy.

Have a firm date specified in the contract of sale, with the option to rescind if it is not met.

EXAMPLE 4

Sue and Russ, parents of two, were handy at making minor home repairs. Since they were planning on having more children, they decided to sell their smaller house and buy a larger one. Russ figured they could afford the move if they bought a handyman's special and fixed it up themselves. A broker showed them a large, older house that was in need of considerable repair. They bought it, figuring that some plaster and lots of paint would transform the handyman's special into a more valuable home. Unfortunately, there were also foundation problems, which affected the entire house. Correcting the structural problems cost Russ and Sue over $5000.

Conclusion: When buying a handyman's special, always hire a structural engineer to inspect the foundation and framing.

EXAMPLE 5

Joyce and Howard had enough of renting and decided to take advantage of the space and tax breaks of surburban living. Since their taste tended toward the modern, they were fascinated by a new, strikingly designed home with lots of glass. The broker advised them to act fact to beat other buyers who were also interested in the house. The broker's list of costs showed that the previous year's heating expense was quite reasonable. Joyce and Howard bought the house and were soon very unhappy. The far-out glass design made it practically impossible to heat the house properly in winter. The previous year's heating bills were reasonable only because the owner had spent the coldest months in a warmer climate.

Conclusions: Beware of high-styled homes unless you explore the practicality of the entire structure with a qualified architect.

Ask questions if common sense tells you that an operating expense such as heating costs is lower than you anticipated.

EXAMPLE 6

Charlene and Bert both worked full-time. Because they had no deductions, they paid sky-high taxes. So, they decided to look for a house. Their broker stressed all

NEVER BUY
UNPRACTICAL
DESIGN!

of the deductions available to homeowners. Without investigating further, Charlene and Bert bought an $85,000 home with 10% down and the balance financed by the developer at 8% per year. Delighted with their interest and property-tax deductions, they broke their existing lease and moved into their new home. Three years later, when Charlene left her job to care for their first baby, Bert's salary barely covered the monthly carrying costs. In addition, they paid $20,000 too much on their impulsive purchase and were forced to sell the house at a huge loss.

Conclusions: Look into the future before you buy something that requires two incomes to maintain.

Take the time to shop around. Do not act on impulse.

Tax savings are not as important as the real value of a home.

Don't be so swayed by the immediate tax advantages that you forget the importance of the purchase price.

EXAMPLE 7

Phil and Barry are bachelors who like the beach. Since they go to the same area almost every summer weekend, they decided to purchase a vacation home in a development near the ocean. They believed this would save them from having to make motel reservations every week. They would also build up some equity. The sales agent told them that if they bought the house, they could rent it out all winter, thus covering all the expenses. Barry thought that half of the $350 per month carrying costs would be too high for his budget, but Phil talked him into buying, reminding him of the sales agent's assurance that rental would be easy. A year later, however, there were no renters in sight. Barry had problems making the payments on his share of the house, and Phil had to put up the shortfall. In addition, it was a poor summer weather-wise, and so they got little use out of the house.

Conclusions: Never buy a vacation home if you cannot afford to maintain it without rental income.

It is usually best not to have multiple owners.

EXAMPLE 8

Karen and Steven were in a hurry to purchase a house because they were expecting their first child. They located a good value in an area they found desirable and on their broker's advice got financing from a local bank for 25 years at 9½%. One year later interest rates dropped considerably, and the couple found that another lending institution would give them a 30-year mortgage at 8½%. This would mean a savings of several thousand dollars over the term of loan along with lower monthly payments. At the closing, however, Karen and Steven had been so excited they did not read all of the terms of their mortgage. There was a large prepayment penalty in the mortgage from the local bank, which stopped them from refinancing on the more attractive terms.

Conclusions: Shop around for lenders just as you would for any service.

Ask about prepayment penalties.

Read what you sign at the closing, and understand what it can mean in the future.

EXAMPLE 9

Irene and Tom were loaded with cash after selling their large family home in Connecticut. They wanted a winter house in Florida, in a prestigious area. Without consulting their lawyer, they signed a binder and put a $25,000 deposit on a house in a development in which a well-known actor had an investment. The aura of prosperity made them feel that they were making a sound investment.

For the summer, Irene and Tom wanted a small lakeside home in New Hampshire. Irene located the perfect development, which was being constructed by a friendly local builder. The basement was not completed, some doors were missing, and the driveway had to be paved. Nevertheless, the builder said that he needed a deposit immediately because other buyers were interested in the home. Tom and Irene gave him a $17,500 deposit, expecting to close the deal and be given title on the house in about two months.

Irene and Tom then retained an excellent attorney to complete the two purchases. The attorney discovered that the prestige community in Florida had gone bankrupt before the streets were paved or the sewer lines hooked up. When the attorney tried to get their deposit refunded, it was impossible to collect from the insolvent development corporation.

On the New Hampshire vacation house, there was a dispute over what the local builder had responsibility to complete. The lawyer will have to sue, and it will be up to a jury to decide what further obligations the local builder has.

Conclusions: Never sign anything unless your attorney has approved it.

Prominent people do not necessarily assure a good investment.

Don't give a deposit directly to a builder. Put all deposits in an escrow account pending completion of the sale.

EXAMPLE 10

Beth and Alan were a busy couple who spent 14 hours a day in their own business. When they decided to buy a house, they contacted one broker and spent only two weekends searching. The development house they chose was lovely, but the couple failed to allot the time to explore the surrounding community. Within two years, a factory had been built directly across the street from the development, and zoning had been downgraded to accommodate commercial enterprises. As a result, the value of homes in their development fell dramatically.

Conclusions: When buying shelter, remember that its value can decline rapidly if the character of the neighborhood changes.

A thorough inspection of a community will usually give advance warning of any imminent changes from residential to commercial zoning.

Appendix I

SINGLE-FAMILY-HOUSE GLOSSARY OF COMMON TERMS

Acceleration Clause
A clause in the mortgage contract that serves to make the entire balance outstanding due and immediately payable if there has been a breach of the mortgage contract by the purchaser.

Abstract of Title
A document ordered by the buyer's attorney for a closing of the sale. It contains a list of all instruments, legal claims, and encumbrances on the property that occurred because of previous Chain of Titles.

Adjustments at Closing
The apportionment between the buyer and the seller, as of the date of the Closing of Title, or expenses such as maintenance, taxes, prepaid charges, and oil.

Amortization
The gradual repayment of a mortgage debt on a payment schedule, which is usually once per month.

Assessed Value
The value placed on realty by an elected or appointed local official. It is usually reported as value of the land and value of the improvements on the land. The assessed value is used to determine the taxes that the community will place on the property.

Building Code   The details of how a building is to be erected in a specific community. Since requirements vary, the ordinance is usually enforced by a local building inspector.

Certificate of Occupancy   A license given by a local official, which permits occupancy of the home. It usually means that the premises have been inspected and construction conforms to the local building code.

Certificate of Satisfaction   A paper showing the discharge of an obligation that has been paid.

Chain of Title   A history of all prior owners of a house, up to the present owner, who have been recorded in public records.

Closing   The final completion of the sale of real property where the balance of money above the down payment is exchanged for the deed.

Closing Statement   A detailed presentation drawn by an attorney, which explains the details of a transfer of title.

Commitment Letter   A letter from a bank or other financial institution that states that a mortgage loan will be extended under specific terms and conditions.

Contract of Sale   A contract that fixes the obligations of the seller and purchaser for the transfer of title to real estate.

Deed   The legal instrument that embodies ownership of property and passes title from the seller to the purchaser.

Deed with Full Covenant   Contains the seller's representation that he owns the property, has the right to sell it to you, and will warrant that there are no defects in the title. Frequently called *warranty deed*.

Down Payment   The amount of money (usually 10% of the purchase price) paid or escrowed on signing of a Contract of Sale. The contract usually contains conditions that must be fulfilled by the seller or else the seller must refund the down payment to the purchaser. Some common conditions are: the obtaining of a mortgage, termite inspection, engineering inspection, and getting clear title.

Easement

The right of one party to use the property of another.

Eminent Domain

The inherent power of a municipality to appropriate private property for the benefit of the public.

Equity

The money interest that an owner holds in a property. Thus, a house worth $80,000 on the open market, with a mortgage debt of $50,000, would have an owner's equity of $30,000.

Escalator Clause

A clause in a lease that provides for increased rental payments in accordance with an index such as the consumer price index. These clauses must be carefully considered because they can dramatically affect monthly charges during an inflationary period.

Escrow Agreement

An agreement in which an agent, usually a bank, broker, or attorney, holds on to a down payment while the conditions in the Contract of Sale are being acted upon. It is generally best to escrow a down payment and thus avoid the potential problems of trying to force the seller to return money because a condition cannot be met.

Fee Simple

Outright ownership of land in the highest degree. The only limitations on this type of ownership are governmental limitations.

Fixtures

Property that is attached to realty in a way that would cause substantial damage if it were removed. For example, a carport, sundeck, brick barbecue, or gazebo.

Going to Contract

The formal signing of a written contract for sale of real property. All of the terms and conditions of the sale are specified in detail, and a date is set for a closing where monies will be exchanged for the deed or other evidence of ownership. At the time of going to contract, a down payment of 10% of the purchase price is given to the seller or an escrow agent.

Indenture	A legal term for a formal, written instrument.

Joint Tenancy	Two or more individuals hold equal title to real property whereby, if one owner dies, his or her interest goes to the surviving owner(s). There is personal liability for all expenses.
Judgment Lien	A lien on property arising out of a lawsuit or other legal proceeding.
Lessee	The tenant in leased space.
Lessor	The landlord in leased space.
Lien	A legal claim on another person's property as security for a debt. There are four common types of liens: *see* **Judgment Lien, Mechanic's Lien, Mortgage Lien, Tax Lien.**
Mechanic's Lien	A legal claim on property by a person who has furnished labor and materials that have improved the property.
Monthly Cash Flow	The monthly expense for heating, electricity, real-estate taxes, school taxes, other taxes, insurance, and mortgage payments.
Mortgage	An instrument that pledges property to a financial institution or a person as security for a loan.
Mortgagee	The lender of funds that are secured by a mortgage.
Mortgage Lien	Pledges a buyer's specific house as collateral for the portion of the purchase price financed.
Mortgagor	The borrower of funds secured by a mortgage.
Net Monthly Cash Flow	The actual cost for utilities, taxes, mortgage, and other expenses after all available tax benefits are subtracted from monthly cash flow.

Personal Property	Everything except the real property that can be subject to ownership.
Points	A disguised form of interest, when a lender requires a set fee from the borrower in advance of the mortgage loan. One point is 1% of the amount of the loan.
Prepayment	A clause in a mortgage contract that requires the mortgagor to pay a penalty if the mortgage is prepaid prior to its maturity. Most mortgage contracts have such a dollar penalty in the first year of the mortgage.
Pro Rata	Divided or assessed proportionally.
Proration	A division of obligations between the buyer and seller at closing.
Purchase-Money Mortgage	A mortgage given by the seller at the time of closing, which takes the place of cash due at the closing.

Quitclaim Deed	The least desirable type of deed because it contains no warranties of any kind. The seller merely conveys whatever interest he or she has in the title to the land to the purchaser.
Real Estate	*See* **Real Property**.
Real Property	This includes the lands, structures on the land, what is under the land, and the airspace over the land. The term *real estate* is used as a synonym for real property.
Recording	Having a written instrument placed in the public records. Deeds, mortgage liens, and other instruments are usually recorded in the county clerk's office or in the county court-house.
RESPA	Real Estate Settlement Procedures Act, which requires a lender to give a good-faith estimate of settlement costs and an informational booklet at the time of submission of a loan application.

Restrictive Covenant A limitation in a deed that requires property to be used or not to be used in some stipulated manner.

Satisfaction of a Mortgage A legal instrument that discharges a mortgage lien. It is often publicly recorded.

S

Settlement Costs The costs paid at a closing to enable the completion of the sale. They include legal fees, recording of mortgage fee, mortgage tax, cost of title search and title insurance, the purchaser's reimbursement of seller's prepaid taxes, and bank charges.

Subject to a Mortgage In the purchase of a piece of property that already has a mortgage, the purchaser assumes the mortgage obligation of the former owner.

Survey An engineering examination of property that identifies its boundaries and the location of structures on the property.

Survivorship The right to share in the untransferred interest of the owner of property after his or her death. The property must have been owned as joint tenants.

Tax Lien The levy of a tax by a government authority on the owner of property.

t

Tenancy by the Entirety A form of ownership of property similar to joint tenancy and based on the concept that husband and wife are one. Upon death of either spouse, his or her interest is transferred to the surviving spouse. Unlike joint tenancy, a spouse may not transfer interest in the property without consent of the other spouse.

Tenants in Common A form of ownership of property where two or more persons own a share in the common property. Shares may be equal or unequal, and upon death an owner's share goe to his or her heirs and not to the other owners. *See* **Joint Tenancy.**

Title   Legal term indicating that the owner of land has the just and legitimate possession of it.

Title Insurance   A special kind of insurance that protects the purchaser of real property against defects in title that may be passed from the seller of the property.

Title Search   An examination of the title of the owner of real property from the public records to determine if it is free and clear of liens and other encumbrances. Such a search is usually necessary before title insurance may be obtained to guard against taking imperfect title from the seller.

W

Warranty Deed   *See* **Deed with Full Covenants.**

Z

Zoning   The wide variety of controls that are exercised over real property by the local community for protection of the public.

Appendix II

VOCABULARY FOR THE HOMEOWNER

ABS. (Acrylonitrile-butadiene-styrene). A plastic from which pipes are made.

Abut. To meet at an end.

Acoustical fiberboard. Low-density fiber material that absorbs sound in the ceiling or wall.

Adapter. Electrical fitting that adjusts an appliance plug to fit into a wall socket.

Adhesives. Glues of various types.

Aggregate. Broken stone, gravel, or sand that forms a substantial part of plaster or concrete.

Air-change. Standard of ventilation that consists of changing the volume of air in a room.

Air-dried timber. Wood in which moisture has come into equilibrium with surrounding air instead of being dried in a kiln.

Air duct. Air passage, usually made of sheet metal, which ventilates a house.

Aluminum paint. Paint made from an aluminum powder that reduces corrosion.

Anchor bolt. Bolt used to attach wood to masonry.

Apron. Panel or board below a window, which projects into a room.

Arris gutter. V-shaped, wooden gutter.

Artificial marble. Made from gypsum plaster.

Artificial stone. Made from special stone that is crushed, mixed with concrete, and colored.

Asbestos shingle. Mixture of cement and asbestos that is often used as siding material.

Asbestos wallboard. Sheets with a high content of asbestos, which consequently are more fire resistant.

Ash. Valuable hardwood used in veneers; colors range from white to light brown.

Ashlar. Square-cut stone that is used in walls or facing.

Asphalt roofing. Lengths of bitumen felt laid in strips along a roof and cut to look like slates.

Axed work. Stone that has been struck with a hammer to show rough marks.

Backfill. Earth, stone, or hard rubbish used for filling excavations after foundation has been built.

Backing. Bricks in a wall that are hidden by the outside *facing bricks.*

Balloon framing. Studs run from foundation to the roofplate; floor joists are nailed to them.

Balusters. Upright supports of a railing or banister.

Baseboard. Molding at the base of a wall, which meets the flooring.

Baseboard heating. Heating units, usually electrical, which are at the base of the walls in a room.

Batt. Blanket-form insulation material installed between wood in the frame.

Bay window. Window that projects beyond the wall in which it was set.

Beam. Support that holds up weight; a girder; may be made of wood or steel.

Beech. Valuable hardwood with spindle-shaped markings.

Bend. Curved length of pipe or tubing.

Bevel. Surface meeting another surface at an angle that is not a right angle.

Bib. Water tap fed from a horizontal pipe instead of from below.

Binder. Cement, tar, bitumen, plaster, or synthetic resin used to join stones or sand.

Birch. One of the hardest woods, it is commonly used in furniture or plywood.

Bitumen. A joining material such as pitch.

Black mortar. A cheap grade of mortar.

Blanket. Insulation material with paper on one or both faces.

Bled timber. Timber from trees tapped for resin; usually cheaper than other timbers and of lesser quality.

Blind floor. Subfloor.

Blistering. Bubbles in a paint surface.

Board foot. Unit of board measurement: 1 foot by 1 foot by 1 inch.

Boiler. Domestic water heater operating on coal, oil, gas, or electricity.

Bolt. Part of a lock that prevents a door from opening.

Bonnet. Roof over a bay window.

Boot. Projection from a concrete beam or floor slab that holds up facing brick.

Braced frame. Wood building frame in which heavy corner posts hold the weight and the studs in between carry no load.

Bridging. Stiffening of joists with small wooden or metal pieces to share carrying the load.

Brown rot. Decay of timber to a brown, soft mass.

Btu (British thermal unit). A measure of heat; the amount of heat required to raise 1 pound of water from 39°F to 40°F.

Building code. Set of rules established by a local area to standardize materials and procedures in construction.

Building inspector. Local official with knowledge of building construction who enforces the building code.

Built-up. Timber beam made of several smaller beams nailed together.

Butt. To meet without overlapping.

BX cable. An electric cable encased in metal.

Cable. The copper wires through which any electric appliance receives power.

Cant molding. Has flat surfaces and no curves.

Cap. Top piece on a post; a cover with internal threads, which screws on the end of a pipe.

Carbonation. Natural, slow, hardening of limestone mortars into stable calcium carbonate.

Carpet-tack strip. Strip of wood with nails in it that is used to hold carpet in place.

Cased frame. Hollow part of a sash window, which contains weights and pulleys.

Casement window. Window that opens on vertical hinges like a door.

Cast stone. Imitation stone used for facing.

Catch bolt. Spring-loaded door lock.

Caulking. Flexible putty used to make seams water- or air-tight.

Ceiling joist. Joist that carries the ceiling beneath it but not the floor above.

Cement. Bond between rock, sand, and other substances; glue.

Certificate. Statement signed by the architect that enables the builder to be paid in installments as work progresses.

Check. Cracks that appear in timber improperly seasoned.

Chestnut. Timber that resembles oak but lacks silver grain; used in fences and gates.

Chimneyback. Wall behind a fireplace.

Chipboards. Artificial wood compressed from wastewood with synthetic resins as binder.

Cinder block. Common building block made of cement and cinder.

Circuit. The complete path of electricity from the power source to an outlet and return.

Circuit breaker. Safety device that interrupts electrical flow.

Circular stair. Spiral staircase.

Circulation. Arrangement and proportion of rooms and spaces to allow proper traffic and airflow.

Cistern. Cold-water storage tank, usually affixed to roof of a house.

Clapboard. Bevel siding commonly used on the outside of wood-framed houses.

Clay tile. Roofing tile.

Cleanout. Soot door for cleaning the ash bin of a fireplace.

Coarse stuff. Material used for the first and second coats of a plaster wall.

Coat. Single layer of paint.

Cock. Valve for controlling a pipeline.

Collar. Ring built around a pipe passing through a roof which ensures watertight fit.

Combination door. Door with an inner removable section; storm door.

Common brick. Locally cheapest brick; not used for facing or to support weight.

Common wall. Party wall.

Composite board. Plywood glued to other material such as an insulation board.

Composite shingles. Imitation shingles made of bitumen.

Concrete block. Grey-colored rectangular block used in constructing foundations and walls; it is considerably stronger than cinder block.

Condensation. Water forming on a surface.

Conditioning. Reducing or increasing the moisture content of wood to the right value.

Conductor. Substance with high conductivity for heat or electricity.

Conduit. Metal or plastic casing around cables; a culvert for carrying water.

Contractor. Person who contracts to do specific work for a specified price.

Convection. Warm fluid or air decreases in density and rises, while cooler fluid or air becomes denser and falls.

Coping. Overhang that protects a wall from rain.

Cornice. Molding at the top of an outside wall which overhangs the wall.

Cost-plus-fixed-fee. Client pays full cost of materials and guarantees contractor a certain percentage profit.

Crawl space. Shallow area between floor and ground in a basementless house.

Crazing. Hairline cracks on the surface of concrete.

Cyclone cellar. A protected storm cellar.

Damper. Metal plate across the flue in a fireplace.

Dead wire. Wire in which no current passes through from power source.

Dead lock. Lock that is worked by keys from both sides.

Degree day. A number that describes the relative coldness of a particular area.

Desiccation of lumber. Drying of lumber in a kiln.

Detector. Device that controls ringing of an alarm in a fire or burglar system.

Dew point. Temperature at which water vapor in air begins to condense.

Dimension shingles. Shingles cut to uniform rather than random width.

Door frame. The surrounding wood or metal of a door that caries it on the hinge.

Doorjamb. Vertical piece forming the side of a door opening.

Doorstop. A catch set in the floor to keep a door from opening too far and damaging a wall.

Dormer. Vertical window coming through a sloping roof and covered by its own roof. Usually used to create more attic space.

Double-hung sash window. Window that opens by raising and lowering.

Dowel. Short, round wooden rod used to hold wooden parts together in such places as a front door.

Downpipe. Vertical pipe that brings water to the ground from roof gutters.

Drain cock. Valve at the lowest point of a water system, which allows it to be periodically drained.

Dressing. Finished building stone.

Drying. Hardening of a coat of paint, varnish, or cement through evaporation or chemical action.

Dry rot. Timber decay due to dampness.

Dry-wall. Ready-made panel used for walls; gypsum board; wallboard.

Ducts. Tubes that carry air to various parts of the house for heating and air conditioning.

Dusting. Wear of a concrete floor caused by excessive water having been mixed in the concrete.

Eave. Overhang section of a sloping roof.

Edge nailing. Hidden nailing of floorboards, etc.

Elbow. Sharp corner in a pipe.

Electric panel box. Cabinet where fuses or circuit breakers are joined; contains main disconnect switch.

Ell. An L-shaped structure.

Enamel paint. A high-gloss paint.

End grain. The rough grain where timber is cut across the grain.

Erosion. Wearing away of paint or caulking through weathering.

Etching. Cutting the surface of glass.

Exhaust shaft. Ventilating passage that removes air.

Expansion joint. Fiber placed between slabs of concrete to prevent cracks from temperature changes.

Expansion tank. Cylinder tank that allows for the expansion of water when heated in a domestic hot-water system.

Exterior-type plywood. Plywood containing moisture-resistant glue.

Face mix. Mixture of cement and crushed stone.

Face putty. Glazier's putty on the surface of glass.

Facing bricks. Selected and textured brick placed over common bricks.

False ceiling. Ceiling built with a gap between it and the floor above; drop ceiling.

Fenestration. Arrangement of windows and other openings in the walls of a building.

Fiberboard. Insulation material formed into sheets.

Finishing coat. Final layer over previous coats.

Fireback. Wall behind a fireplace.

Firebrick. Brick made to resist heat.

Fire point. Temperature at which a substance ignites.

Fire wall. A division wall made of fireproof material and intended to resist the spread of fire.

Fittings. Various couplings made for connecting pipes.

Flagstone. Sandstone that splits into flat sheets; used on walks and patios.

Flash. To make a weathertight joint.

Flashing. Sheet metal used around doors, chimneys, and windows to prevent water seepage.

Flat finish. A finish with reduced gloss.

Floor framing. Common joists.

Floor plan. A layout of a building by room.

Flue. Passage for smoke in a chimney.

Footing. Concrete-base foundation of a wall or chimney.

Frame. Timber members of a house.

Frontage. Length of house running along the road.

Frost line. Lowest level that earth freezes in a particular area.

Furring. Wood strips fastened to leave an airspace between brick and plaster.

Fuse box. Cabinet housing fuses.

Gable. Triangular part of the end wall of a building with a sloping roof.

Garderobe. Small room in which clothing or other items are stored.

Gatepost. Wooden or metal post on which a gate hinge is fixed.

Girder. Main beam supporting a house.

Girt. Small girder.

Glass bricks. Blocks of glass used to admit diffused light.

Gloss. Reflection of light on a painted surface.

Grade. Quality or class of timber; also the slope or pitch of ground about a house.

Grading. Moving the soil to slope away from the foundation of a house for drainage.

Grain. General direction and arrangement of the fibers in wood.

Grille. Open metal or wood screen.

Ground. To link an electrical system to the earth.

Gutter. Open channel along the roof eave that removes rainwater.

Gypsum. The raw material for plaster.

Grout. Liquefied mortar put into narrow masonry joints; often used in bathroom tile.

Gypsum plasterboard. Common interior-wall material that comes in sheets and is attached to framing.

Hand. Location of hinges on either the left or right side of a door.

Handrail. Rail at the top of a balcony.

Hang. To fit a door or window in its frame on hinges.

Hardboard. Inexpensive substitute for wood made of small wood fibers bound by adhesive.

Hardwoods. Timber from deciduous trees, which shed their leaves in the fall.

Head. Upper horizontal strip of a door or window frame.

Hearth. Floor of a fireplace.

Heel. Part of a beam resting on a support.
Hew. To shape wood with a hatchet or ax.
Hickory. An expensive, strong timber used in ladder rungs.
Hip. The outstanding edge formed by the meeting of two roof surfaces.
Hollow tile. Building blocks made of hard clay.
Hot wires. Electric wires that conduct power.
Hue. Shade of a color.

I-beam. Steel girder that resembles the letter *I*.
Incise. To cut or carve stone.
Incrustation. Hard lime or other materials that become deposited on water pipes or conduits.
Inlaid parquet. Flooring glued in blocks to a wood backing.
Inspection certificate. Document from a local building authority stating that a structure satisfies the local building code.
Insulation. Material that prevents the conduction of heat, sound, or electricity.
Ironwork. Decorative wrought or cast iron.

Jamb. Vertical piece forming the side of the frame of a door or window.
Joint. Mortar between adjacent bricks or stone.
Joint tape. Paper tape fixed over the seams between wallboards.
Joists. Wood or steel beams that directly support a floor.
Junction box. Metal box that covers the joining of house wiring.

Keystone. Wedge-shaped stone at the crown of an arch.
Kickplate. Metal or plastic plate at the bottom of a door to protect it.
Kiln drying. Baking of timber to season it.
Knee. Sharp right-angle bend in a pipe; elbow.
Knot. Place in a tree trunk from which a branch has grown; knots reduce the strength in wood.

Lally column. Concrete-filled metal column used to support beams.
Laminate. To impregnate with synthetic resin.
Lath. Metal mesh secured to a frame to serve as a base for plaster.
Lattice window. Window with small panes of glass.
Leader. Metal pipe that carries rainwater from the butter to the ground.
Level. To set in a straight edge.
Lightning panel. Cutout box for protecting lighting circuits.
Lintel. Small beam over a door or window carrying the load above it.
Lip. A band.
Live wire. A conductor with electrical power in it.
Load-bearing wall. Wall that supports weight in a house.
Loft. Storage space under a roof.
Louver. Opening with horizontal slats that allows in air and excludes rain; usually found in attics.
Lug. Small projection from a frame or pipe to enable it to be attached or fixed in place.

Made-up ground. Ground that has been raised by fill.

Main. Community supply pipe for water.

Masonry. Stone-wall or brick building.

Medium. Liquid part of a paint or enamel.

Mica. Mineral that can be cut thin enough as to be transparent; very good electrical insulators.

Millwork. Woodwork made and partly assembled at the mill.

Mismatching. A bad fit in grain or size at a joint.

Moisture barrier. Waterproof material that prevents moisture from forming; a vapor barrier.

Molding. Wooden strips used as ornamentation.

Mortar. Mixture of portland cement, sand, and water used for laying bricks.

Mortice. Rectangular slot cut in wood into which a lock is fixed.

Mullion. Thin bars separating windowpanes.

Neutralizing. Preparing concrete surfaces for painting.

Newel. Upright post that supports a handrail.

Nipple. Short pipe threaded outside at both ends used for coupling pipes internally.

Notching. Joining two timbers by cutting part out of each.

Offset. Ledge in a wall.

Open-grained. Wood of coarse texture.

Outlet. Electrical socket.

Overhang. A projection of a roof beyond a wall.

Overhead door. Door that is lifted up and slipped into a horizontal position.

Pane. Sheet of glass between glazing bars.

Panel box. Central electric cutout box containing fuses or circuit breakers.

Parapet. Low wall guarding the edge of a roof or balcony.

Parquet. Hardwood blocks glued to a wooden floor and polished.

Party wall. Wall between two buildings which they use in common.

Pebble dash. External plaster surfaced with clean pebbles.

Pet cock. Small valve that is opened to release air from the upper part of a water pipe.

Pier. Short masonry buttress.

Pitch. Ratio of the height of a house to the span of the roof.

Plaster. Substance that is applied wet to walls and ceilings, which later hardens.

Plasterboard. Rigid interior wallboard made from gypsum coated with heavy paper.

Platform frame. Frame of a house in which each floor is supported by studs only one story tall.

Plug. Electrical connection that fits into the socket.

Plumb. Vertical.

Plywood. Wood sheets made of three or more thin layers glued together.

Pocket piece. Piece at the foot of a window that can be removed to string a new sash cord.

Pores. Small round holes on the end grain of hardwood.

Post. Vertical support thicker than a stud in a frame.

Primer. First coat of paint on new metal or wood.

Quarter bend. A 90° bend in pipe.

Quarter-round. Molding like a quarter circle.

Radiant heating. Heating by radiation from the surface.

Rafter. Sloping timber extending from the ridge of a roof to the eave that supports the roof.

Rag felt. Bitumen felt.

Rain leader. A downpipe that collects water from eave gutters.

Receptacle. A socket outlet.

Reconstructed stone. Cast stone.

Refractory mortar. Mortar used for setting boilers or furnaces.

Reflective insulation. Aluminum-foil-covered insulation material.

Register. Damper that regulates the volume of warm air passing into different rooms.

Reinforced concrete. Poured concrete with steel inside it to add strength.

Rendering. Applying coarse stuff to a wall.

Return. Usually a pipe by which hot water leaves a boiler, heats the radiators, and returns to be reheated.

Ridge. Apex of a roof along a horizontal line.

Ridgeboard. Horizontal plank along the roof line where rafters meet.

Rip. To cut timber parallel to the grain.

Rise. Vertical height of a roof.

Rot. Decay of timber.

Rule. A straightedge of any length.

Rustic brick. Facing brick on which the face has been roughened.

Saddle. Board fixed under a door and projecting on each side of the threshold.

Saddle roof. Pitched roof with gables.

Safety glass. Glass toughened by heat so that it granulates when struck.

Sash. Window framing of a sash window.

Scale. Deposit formed by hard water.

Screwed pipe. The cheapest domestic pipe; made of steel with taper thread.

Sealed system. Heating system sealed from air to prevent corrosion.

Seconds. Second-quality material.

Secret nailing. Method of nailing so that the nail is not seen on the surface; blind nailing.

Septic tank. Purifier for sewage where no sewer is available.

Setback. Withdrawal of the upper floors from the building line.

Setting. Hardening of concrete, mortar, or plaster.

Sewer trap. Device that prevents sewer gas from seeping into the house.

Shakes. Hand-split shingles, usually of cedar.

Sheathing. Material nailed to exterior studs to form a base for the finish.

Shed roof. A lean-to roof.

Shingle. Rectangular building material laid in overlapping rows on the exterior of a house.

Shoe. A length at the bottom of a downpipe that directs water away from the foundation.

Short circuit. Faulty electrical connection that causes fuses of circuit breakers to cut out.

Siding. Any wall cladding except brick or stone.

Sill. Lowest wooden member of a building or window frame.

Skylight. Roof light.

Slab floor. Reinforced concrete floor.

Slate roof. Roof made of natural stone that splits easily into thin sheets and is attached like shingles.

Slop sink. Low sink large enough to accommodate a bucket under the tap.

Soffit. Undersurface of a cornice, stair, beam, arch, or other part of a house.

Softwoods. Evergreen trees, which do not shed leaves in winter.

Soil pipe. Vertical pipe in a plumbing system that takes sewage down from all parts of the house.

Sole plate. Horizontal timber on which wall studs rest.

Solid door. Solid-core door that has no hollow.

Splice. Joint between timbers; usually reinforced on each side by wood or steel plates bolted together.

Spotting. Defect in a painted surface that may cause a different color or gloss.

Stop cock. Valve in a gas or water-supply pipe.

Stucco. Exterior finish of portland cement.

Stud. Intermediate vertical members in a framed house.

Subfloor. Rough flooring laid on the joists.

Sump pump. Small-capacity pump that empties water from basements.

Suspended ceiling. False ceiling.

Sweating. Condensation that forms on pipes.

Tack. Small, sharp nail with a large head.

Tar-gravel roof. Low-cost roof covering of hot tar or pitch covered with gravel.

Termite shield. Metal sheet placed below any wood that prevents termites from entering the house.

Terra cotta. Glazed, baked clay made into brick or tile and used for roofing, facing, or ornamentation.

Three-prong plug. Plug with two prongs for power and a third for an earth ground.

Toggle bolt. Fastening device that spreads out after being inserted in a hole.

Tolerance. Allowable range of variation.
Tongue-and-groove joint. Method of joining boards where a straight tongue is on one board and a groove on the other.
Trap. V-shaped bend in a pipe.
Trim. Interior facing material.

Undercoat. Any coat applied after priming but before the finishing coat.

Valley. Intersection between two sloping sides of a roof.
Valve. Device that opens and closes to regulate flow.
Vault. Arched roof.
Veneer. Thin layer of wood used as a facing to cover up a core.
Ventilation pipe. Stack with an open end that permits air change.
Vitrified pipe. Ceramic pipe often used for underground drainage.
Voltage. Electrical pressure.

Wainscot. Wood paneling on the lower part of walls.
Wallboard. Fabricated building boards made for surfacing of walls or ceilings.
Warp. Any distortion of wood such as twisting.
Water table. Projection fixed to the foot of a wall to divert rainwater.
Watt. Power obtained from 1 ampere flowing at the pressure of 1 volt.
Weathering. Chemical breakup of wood due to exposure to the elements.
Weephole. Small opening that allows water to escape.
Wormhole. Any hole bored by insects.

Appendix III

MONTHLY MORTGAGE COSTS PER THOUSAND DOLLARS INCLUDING INTEREST

To use these tables, locate the interest rate on your mortgage along the top line and the term of the mortgage in the left-hand column. The number at the intersection is your monthly cost per thousand dollars for principal and interest. Multiply the number times the thousands of dollars in your mortgage.

Example: A $51,000 mortgage at 8½% for a term of 20 years:
$$\$8.68 \times 51 = \$442.68/\text{month.}$$

Example: A $32,000 mortgage at 7¼% for a term of 30 years:
$$\$6.83 \times 32 = \$218.56/\text{month.}$$

AMORTIZATION TABLES

MONTHLY INSTALLMENT PER THOUSAND DOLLARS INCLUDING INTEREST AT—

Term of Mortgage Years	Months	No. of Payments	5%	5¼%	5½%	5¾%	6%	6¼%	6½%	6¾%	7%	7¼%	7½%	7¾%	8%	8¼%	8½%	8¾%	9%	9¼%	9½%	9¾%
40	0	480	4.83	4.99	5.16	5.33	5.51	5.68	5.86	6.04	6.22	6.40	6.59	6.77	6.96	7.15	7.34	7.53	7.72	7.91	8.11	8.30
39	11	479	4.83	5.00	5.17	5.34	5.51	5.69	5.86	6.04	6.22	6.40	6.59	6.77	6.96	7.15	7.34	7.53	7.72	7.91	8.11	8.30
39	10	478	4.83	5.00	5.17	5.34	5.51	5.69	5.86	6.04	6.22	6.41	6.59	6.78	6.96	7.15	7.34	7.53	7.72	7.91	8.11	8.30
39	9	477	4.84	5.00	5.17	5.34	5.52	5.69	5.87	6.05	6.23	6.41	6.59	6.78	6.96	7.15	7.34	7.53	7.72	7.92	8.11	8.30
39	8	476	4.84	5.01	5.17	5.35	5.52	5.69	5.87	6.05	6.23	6.41	6.59	6.78	6.97	7.16	7.34	7.53	7.73	7.92	8.11	8.31
39	7	475	4.84	5.01	5.18	5.35	5.52	5.70	5.87	6.05	6.23	6.41	6.60	6.78	6.97	7.16	7.35	7.54	7.73	7.92	8.11	8.31
39	6	474	4.85	5.01	5.18	5.35	5.52	5.70	5.88	6.06	6.23	6.42	6.60	6.78	6.97	7.16	7.35	7.54	7.73	7.92	8.11	8.31
39	5	473	4.85	5.02	5.18	5.35	5.53	5.70	5.88	6.06	6.23	6.42	6.60	6.79	6.97	7.16	7.35	7.54	7.73	7.92	8.11	8.31
39	4	472	4.85	5.02	5.19	5.36	5.53	5.70	5.88	6.06	6.24	6.42	6.60	6.79	6.97	7.16	7.35	7.54	7.73	7.92	8.12	8.31
39	3	471	4.86	5.02	5.19	5.36	5.53	5.71	5.88	6.06	6.24	6.42	6.61	6.79	6.98	7.16	7.35	7.54	7.73	7.92	8.12	8.31
39	2	470	4.86	5.03	5.19	5.36	5.54	5.71	5.89	6.06	6.24	6.43	6.61	6.79	6.98	7.17	7.35	7.54	7.74	7.93	8.12	8.32
39	1	469	4.86	5.03	5.20	5.37	5.54	5.71	5.89	6.07	6.25	6.43	6.61	6.79	6.98	7.17	7.36	7.55	7.74	7.93	8.12	8.32
39	0	468	4.87	5.03	5.20	5.37	5.54	5.72	5.89	6.07	6.25	6.43	6.61	6.80	6.98	7.17	7.36	7.55	7.74	7.93	8.12	8.32
38	11	467	4.87	5.03	5.20	5.37	5.54	5.72	5.89	6.07	6.25	6.43	6.62	6.80	6.99	7.17	7.36	7.55	7.74	7.93	8.13	8.32
38	10	466	4.87	5.04	5.21	5.38	5.55	5.72	5.90	6.07	6.25	6.43	6.62	6.80	6.99	7.17	7.36	7.55	7.74	7.93	8.13	8.32
38	9	465	4.88	5.04	5.21	5.38	5.55	5.72	5.90	6.08	6.26	6.44	6.62	6.80	6.99	7.18	7.36	7.55	7.74	7.94	8.13	8.32
38	8	464	4.88	5.04	5.21	5.38	5.55	5.73	5.90	6.08	6.26	6.44	6.62	6.81	6.99	7.18	7.37	7.56	7.75	7.94	8.13	8.33
38	7	463	4.88	5.05	5.22	5.38	5.56	5.73	5.91	6.08	6.26	6.44	6.62	6.81	6.99	7.18	7.37	7.56	7.75	7.94	8.13	8.33
38	6	462	4.89	5.05	5.22	5.39	5.56	5.73	5.91	6.09	6.26	6.45	6.63	6.81	7.00	7.18	7.37	7.56	7.75	7.94	8.13	8.33
38	5	461	4.89	5.05	5.22	5.39	5.56	5.74	5.91	6.09	6.27	6.45	6.63	6.81	7.00	7.19	7.37	7.56	7.75	7.94	8.14	8.33
38	4	460	4.89	5.06	5.23	5.39	5.57	5.74	5.91	6.09	6.27	6.45	6.63	6.82	7.00	7.19	7.38	7.56	7.75	7.95	8.14	8.33
38	3	459	4.90	5.06	5.23	5.40	5.57	5.74	5.92	6.09	6.27	6.65	6.63	6.82	7.00	7.19	7.38	7.57	7.76	7.95	8.14	8.33
38	2	458	4.90	5.07	5.23	5.40	5.57	5.74	5.92	6.10	6.28	6.46	6.64	6.82	7.00	7.19	7.38	7.57	7.76	7.95	8.14	8.33
38	1	457	4.90	5.07	5.24	5.40	5.58	5.75	5.92	6.10	6.28	6.46	6.64	6.82	7.01	7.19	7.38	7.57	7.76	7.95	8.14	8.34
38	0	456	4.91	5.07	5.24	5.41	5.58	5.75	5.93	6.10	6.28	6.46	6.64	6.83	7.01	7.20	7.38	7.57	7.76	7.95	8.15	8.34
37	11	455	4.91	5.08	5.24	5.41	5.58	5.75	5.93	6.11	6.28	6.46	6.64	6.83	7.01	7.20	7.39	7.57	7.76	7.95	8.15	8.34
37	10	454	4.92	5.08	5.25	5.41	5.58	5.76	5.93	6.11	6.29	6.47	6.65	6.83	7.01	7.20	7.39	7.58	7.77	7.96	8.15	8.34
37	9	453	4.92	5.08	5.25	5.42	5.59	5.76	5.93	6.11	6.29	6.47	6.65	6.83	7.02	7.20	7.39	7.58	7.77	7.96	8.15	8.34
37	8	452	4.92	5.09	5.25	5.42	5.59	5.76	5.94	6.11	6.29	6.47	6.65	6.84	7.02	7.21	7.39	7.58	7.77	7.96	8.15	8.35
37	7	451	4.93	5.09	5.26	5.42	5.59	5.77	5.94	6.12	6.29	6.47	6.66	6.84	7.02	7.21	7.39	7.58	7.77	7.96	8.15	8.35
37	6	450	4.93	5.09	5.26	5.43	5.60	5.77	5.94	6.12	6.30	6.48	6.66	6.84	7.02	7.21	7.40	7.58	7.77	7.96	8.16	8.35
37	5	449	4.93	5.10	5.26	5.43	5.60	5.77	5.95	6.12	6.30	6.48	6.66	6.84	7.03	7.21	7.40	7.59	7.78	7.97	8.16	8.35

Yr	Mo	Mos																				
37	4	448	4.94	5.10	5.27	5.43	5.60	5.78	5.95	6.13	6.30	6.48	6.66	6.85	7.03	7.21	7.40	7.59	7.78	7.97	8.16	8.35
37	3	447	4.94	5.10	5.27	5.44	5.61	5.78	5.95	6.13	6.31	6.49	6.67	6.85	7.03	7.22	7.40	7.59	7.78	7.97	8.16	8.35
37	2	446	4.94	5.11	5.27	5.44	5.61	5.78	5.96	6.13	6.31	6.49	6.67	6.85	7.03	7.22	7.41	7.59	7.78	7.97	8.16	8.36
37	1	445	4.95	5.11	5.28	5.44	5.61	5.79	5.96	6.14	6.31	6.49	6.67	6.85	7.04	7.22	7.41	7.60	7.78	7.97	8.17	8.36
37	0	444	4.95	5.12	5.28	5.45	5.62	5.79	5.96	6.14	6.32	6.49	6.67	6.86	7.04	7.22	7.41	7.60	7.79	7.98	8.17	8.36
36	11	443	4.96	5.12	5.28	5.45	5.62	5.79	5.97	6.14	6.32	6.50	6.68	6.86	7.04	7.23	7.41	7.60	7.79	7.98	8.17	8.36
36	10	442	4.96	5.12	5.29	5.46	5.62	5.80	5.97	6.14	6.32	6.50	6.68	6.86	7.05	7.23	7.42	7.60	7.79	7.98	8.17	8.36
36	9	441	4.96	5.13	5.29	5.46	5.63	5.80	5.97	6.15	6.32	6.50	6.68	6.86	7.05	7.23	7.42	7.61	7.79	7.98	8.17	8.37
36	8	440	4.97	5.13	5.30	5.47	5.63	5.80	5.98	6.15	6.33	6.51	6.69	6.87	7.05	7.23	7.42	7.61	7.80	7.99	8.18	8.37
36	7	439	4.97	5.13	5.30	5.47	5.64	5.81	5.98	6.15	6.33	6.51	6.69	6.87	7.05	7.24	7.42	7.61	7.80	7.99	8.18	8.37
36	6	438	4.98	5.14	5.30	5.47	5.64	5.81	5.98	6.16	6.33	6.51	6.69	6.87	7.06	7.24	7.43	7.61	7.80	7.99	8.18	8.37
36	5	437	4.98	5.14	5.31	5.48	5.64	5.81	5.99	6.16	6.34	6.52	6.70	6.88	7.06	7.24	7.43	7.62	7.81	7.99	8.18	8.37
36	4	436	4.98	5.15	5.31	5.48	5.65	5.82	5.99	6.16	6.34	6.52	6.70	6.88	7.06	7.25	7.43	7.62	7.81	7.99	8.18	8.38
36	3	435	4.99	5.15	5.31	5.48	5.65	5.82	5.99	6.17	6.34	6.52	6.70	6.88	7.07	7.25	7.44	7.62	7.81	8.00	8.19	8.38
36	2	434	4.99	5.15	5.32	5.48	5.65	5.82	6.00	6.17	6.35	6.52	6.70	6.88	7.07	7.25	7.44	7.62	7.81	8.00	8.19	8.38
36	1	433	5.00	5.16	5.32	5.49	5.66	5.83	6.00	6.17	6.35	6.53	6.71	6.89	7.07	7.25	7.44	7.62	7.81	8.00	8.19	8.38
36	0	432	5.00	5.16	5.33	5.49	5.66	5.83	6.00	6.18	6.35	6.53	6.71	6.89	7.07	7.26	7.44	7.63	7.81	8.00	8.19	8.38
35	11	431	5.00	5.17	5.33	5.50	5.66	5.83	6.01	6.18	6.36	6.53	6.71	6.89	7.08	7.26	7.44	7.63	7.82	8.01	8.20	8.39
35	10	430	5.01	5.17	5.33	5.50	5.67	5.84	6.01	6.18	6.36	6.54	6.72	6.90	7.08	7.26	7.45	7.63	7.82	8.01	8.20	8.39
35	9	429	5.01	5.17	5.34	5.50	5.67	5.84	6.01	6.19	6.36	6.54	6.72	6.90	7.08	7.26	7.45	7.63	7.82	8.01	8.20	8.39
35	8	428	5.02	5.18	5.34	5.51	5.68	5.85	6.02	6.19	6.37	6.54	6.72	6.90	7.08	7.27	7.45	7.64	7.82	8.01	8.20	8.39
35	7	427	5.02	5.18	5.35	5.51	5.68	5.85	6.02	6.19	6.37	6.55	6.72	6.90	7.09	7.27	7.45	7.64	7.83	8.02	8.20	8.39
35	6	426	5.03	5.19	5.35	5.52	5.68	5.85	6.02	6.20	6.37	6.55	6.73	6.91	7.09	7.27	7.46	7.64	7.83	8.02	8.21	8.40
35	5	425	5.03	5.19	5.35	5.52	5.69	5.86	6.03	6.20	6.38	6.55	6.73	6.91	7.09	7.28	7.46	7.65	7.83	8.02	8.21	8.40
35	4	424	5.03	5.20	5.36	5.52	5.69	5.86	6.03	6.20	6.38	6.56	6.73	6.91	7.10	7.28	7.46	7.65	7.83	8.02	8.21	8.40
35	3	423	5.04	5.20	5.36	5.53	5.70	5.86	6.04	6.21	6.38	6.56	6.74	6.92	7.10	7.28	7.47	7.65	7.84	8.02	8.21	8.40
35	2	422	5.04	5.20	5.37	5.53	5.70	5.87	6.04	6.21	6.39	6.56	6.74	6.92	7.10	7.28	7.47	7.65	7.84	8.03	8.22	8.41
35	1	421	5.05	5.21	5.37	5.54	5.70	5.87	6.04	6.22	6.39	6.57	6.74	6.92	7.10	7.29	7.47	7.66	7.84	8.03	8.22	8.41
35	0	420	5.05	5.21	5.38	5.54	5.71	5.88	6.05	6.22	6.39	6.57	6.75	6.93	7.11	7.29	7.47	7.66	7.84	8.03	8.22	8.41
34	11	419	5.06	5.22	5.38	5.54	5.71	5.88	6.05	6.22	6.40	6.57	6.75	6.93	7.11	7.29	7.48	7.66	7.85	8.04	8.22	8.41
34	10	418	5.06	5.22	5.38	5.55	5.71	5.88	6.05	6.23	6.40	6.58	6.75	6.93	7.11	7.30	7.48	7.66	7.85	8.04	8.23	8.42
34	9	417	5.07	5.23	5.39	5.55	5.72	5.89	6.06	6.23	6.40	6.58	6.76	6.94	7.12	7.30	7.48	7.67	7.85	8.04	8.23	8.42
34	8	416	5.07	5.23	5.39	5.56	5.72	5.89	6.06	6.23	6.41	6.58	6.76	6.94	7.12	7.30	7.49	7.67	7.86	8.04	8.23	8.42
34	7	415	5.07	5.23	5.40	5.56	5.73	5.90	6.07	6.24	6.41	6.59	6.76	6.94	7.12	7.31	7.49	7.67	7.86	8.05	8.23	8.42
34	6	414	5.08	5.24	5.40	5.57	5.73	5.90	6.07	6.24	6.42	6.59	6.77	6.95	7.13	7.31	7.49	7.68	7.86	8.05	8.24	8.43
34	5	413	5.08	5.24	5.41	5.57	5.74	5.90	6.07	6.25	6.42	6.59	6.77	6.95	7.13	7.31	7.49	7.68	7.86	8.05	8.24	8.43
34	4	412	5.09	5.25	5.41	5.57	5.74	5.91	6.08	6.25	6.42	6.60	6.77	6.95	7.13	7.31	7.50	7.68	7.87	8.05	8.24	8.43
34	3	411	5.09	5.25	5.41	5.58	5.74	5.91	6.08	6.25	6.43	6.60	6.78	6.96	7.14	7.32	7.50	7.68	7.87	8.06	8.24	8.43

AMORTIZATION TABLES (Continued)

Term of Mortgage		No. of Pay-ments	MONTHLY INSTALLMENT PER THOUSAND DOLLARS INCLUDING INTEREST AT—																			
Years	Months		5%	5¼%	5½%	5¾%	6%	6¼%	6½%	6¾%	7%	7¼%	7½%	7¾%	8%	8¼%	8½%	8¾%	9%	9¼%	9½%	9¾%
34	2	410	5.10	5.26	5.42	5.58	5.75	5.92	6.09	6.26	6.43	6.61	6.78	6.96	7.14	7.32	7.50	7.69	7.87	8.06	8.25	8.44
34	1	409	5.10	5.26	5.42	5.59	5.75	5.92	6.09	6.26	6.43	6.61	6.79	6.96	7.14	7.32	7.51	7.69	7.88	8.06	8.25	8.44
34	0	408	5.11	5.27	5.43	5.59	5.76	5.92	6.09	6.26	6.44	6.61	6.79	6.97	7.15	7.33	7.51	7.69	7.88	8.06	8.25	8.44
33	11	407	5.11	5.27	5.43	5.60	5.76	5.93	6.10	6.27	6.44	6.62	6.79	6.97	7.15	7.33	7.51	7.70	7.88	8.07	8.25	8.44
33	10	406	5.12	5.28	5.44	5.60	5.77	5.93	6.10	6.27	6.45	6.62	6.80	6.97	7.15	7.33	7.52	7.70	7.88	8.07	8.26	8.45
33	9	405	5.12	5.28	5.44	5.60	5.77	5.94	6.11	6.28	6.45	6.62	6.80	6.98	7.16	7.34	7.52	7.70	7.89	8.07	8.26	8.45
33	8	404	5.13	5.29	5.45	5.61	5.77	5.94	6.11	6.28	6.45	6.63	6.80	6.98	7.16	7.34	7.52	7.71	7.89	8.08	8.26	8.45
33	7	403	5.13	5.29	5.45	5.61	5.78	5.95	6.11	6.28	6.46	6.63	6.81	6.98	7.16	7.34	7.53	7.71	7.89	8.08	8.27	8.45
33	6	402	5.14	5.29	5.46	5.62	5.78	5.95	6.12	6.29	6.46	6.64	6.81	6.99	7.17	7.35	7.53	7.71	7.90	8.08	8.27	8.46
33	5	401	5.14	5.30	5.46	5.62	5.79	5.95	6.12	6.29	6.47	6.64	6.81	6.99	7.17	7.35	7.53	7.71	7.90	8.08	8.27	8.46
33	4	400	5.15	5.30	5.46	5.63	5.79	5.96	6.13	6.30	6.47	6.64	6.82	7.00	7.17	7.35	7.54	7.72	7.90	8.09	8.27	8.46
33	3	399	5.15	5.31	5.47	5.63	5.80	5.96	6.13	6.30	6.47	6.65	6.82	7.00	7.18	7.36	7.54	7.72	7.91	8.09	8.28	8.47
33	2	398	5.16	5.31	5.47	5.64	5.80	5.97	6.14	6.31	6.48	6.65	6.83	7.00	7.18	7.36	7.54	7.73	7.91	8.09	8.28	8.47
33	1	397	5.16	5.32	5.48	5.64	5.81	5.97	6.14	6.31	6.48	6.66	6.83	7.01	7.19	7.36	7.55	7.73	7.91	8.10	8.28	8.47
33	0	396	5.17	5.32	5.48	5.65	5.81	5.98	6.14	6.31	6.49	6.66	6.83	7.01	7.19	7.37	7.55	7.73	7.92	8.10	8.29	8.47
32	11	395	5.17	5.33	5.49	5.65	5.82	5.98	6.15	6.32	6.49	6.66	6.84	7.01	7.19	7.37	7.55	7.74	7.92	8.10	8.29	8.48
32	10	394	5.18	5.33	5.49	5.66	5.82	5.99	6.15	6.32	6.49	6.67	6.84	7.02	7.20	7.38	7.56	7.74	7.92	8.11	8.29	8.48
32	9	393	5.18	5.34	5.50	5.66	5.82	5.99	6.16	6.33	6.50	6.67	6.85	7.02	7.20	7.38	7.56	7.74	7.93	8.11	8.30	8.48
32	8	392	5.19	5.34	5.50	5.67	5.83	6.00	6.16	6.33	6.50	6.68	6.85	7.03	7.20	7.38	7.56	7.75	7.93	8.11	8.30	8.49
32	7	391	5.19	5.35	5.51	5.67	5.83	6.00	6.17	6.34	6.51	6.68	6.85	7.03	7.21	7.39	7.57	7.75	7.93	8.12	8.30	8.49
32	6	390	5.20	5.35	5.51	5.68	5.84	6.00	6.17	6.34	6.51	6.68	6.86	7.03	7.21	7.39	7.57	7.75	7.94	8.12	8.30	8.49
32	5	389	5.20	5.36	5.52	5.68	5.84	6.01	6.18	6.35	6.52	6.69	6.86	7.04	7.22	7.39	7.57	7.76	7.94	8.12	8.31	8.49
32	4	388	5.21	5.37	5.52	5.69	5.85	6.01	6.18	6.35	6.52	6.69	6.87	7.04	7.22	7.40	7.58	7.76	7.94	8.13	8.31	8.50
32	3	387	5.21	5.37	5.53	5.69	5.85	6.02	6.19	6.35	6.52	6.70	6.87	7.05	7.22	7.40	7.58	7.76	7.95	8.13	8.31	8.50
32	2	386	5.22	5.38	5.53	5.69	5.86	6.02	6.19	6.36	6.53	6.70	6.88	7.05	7.23	7.41	7.59	7.77	7.95	8.13	8.32	8.50
32	1	385	5.22	5.38	5.54	5.70	5.86	6.03	6.20	6.36	6.53	6.71	6.88	7.05	7.23	7.41	7.59	7.77	7.95	8.14	8.32	8.51
32	0	384	5.23	5.39	5.55	5.71	5.87	6.03	6.20	6.37	6.54	6.71	6.88	7.06	7.24	7.41	7.59	7.77	7.96	8.14	8.32	8.51
31	11	383	5.24	5.39	5.55	5.71	5.87	6.04	6.20	6.37	6.54	6.71	6.89	7.06	7.24	7.42	7.60	7.78	7.96	8.14	8.33	8.51
31	10	382	5.24	5.40	5.56	5.72	5.88	6.04	6.21	6.38	6.55	6.72	6.89	7.07	7.24	7.42	7.60	7.78	7.96	8.15	8.33	8.52
31	9	381	5.25	5.40	5.56	5.72	5.88	6.05	6.21	6.38	6.55	6.72	6.90	7.07	7.25	7.43	7.60	7.79	7.97	8.15	8.33	8.52
31	8	380	5.25	5.41	5.57	5.73	5.89	6.05	6.22	6.39	6.56	6.73	6.90	7.08	7.25	7.43	7.61	7.79	7.97	8.15	8.34	8.52

Yr	Mo	No																				
31	7	379	5.26	5.41	5.57	5.73	5.89	6.06	6.22	6.39	6.56	6.73	6.91	7.08	7.26	7.43	7.61	7.79	7.97	8.16	8.34	8.53
31	6	378	5.26	5.42	5.58	5.74	5.90	6.06	6.23	6.40	6.57	6.74	6.91	7.08	7.26	7.44	7.62	7.80	7.98	8.16	8.34	8.53
31	5	377	5.27	5.43	5.58	5.74	5.91	6.07	6.23	6.40	6.57	6.74	6.91	7.09	7.26	7.44	7.62	7.80	7.98	8.16	8.35	8.53
31	4	376	5.28	5.43	5.59	5.75	5.91	6.07	6.24	6.41	6.58	6.75	6.92	7.09	7.27	7.45	7.62	7.80	7.99	8.17	8.35	8.54
31	3	375	5.28	5.44	5.59	5.75	5.92	6.08	6.24	6.41	6.58	6.75	6.92	7.10	7.27	7.45	7.63	7.81	7.99	8.17	8.36	8.54
31	2	374	5.29	5.44	5.60	5.76	5.92	6.08	6.25	6.42	6.59	6.76	6.93	7.10	7.28	7.45	7.63	7.81	7.99	8.18	8.36	8.54
31	1	373	5.29	5.45	5.61	5.77	5.93	6.09	6.25	6.42	6.59	6.76	6.93	7.11	7.28	7.46	7.64	7.82	8.00	8.18	8.36	8.55
31	0	372	5.30	5.45	5.61	5.77	5.93	6.10	6.26	6.43	6.60	6.77	6.94	7.11	7.29	7.46	7.64	7.82	8.00	8.18	8.37	8.55
30	11	371	5.30	5.46	5.62	5.78	5.94	6.10	6.27	6.43	6.60	6.77	6.94	7.12	7.29	7.47	7.65	7.82	8.01	8.19	8.37	8.55
30	10	370	5.31	5.47	5.62	5.78	5.94	6.11	6.27	6.44	6.61	6.78	6.95	7.12	7.30	7.47	7.65	7.83	8.01	8.19	8.37	8.56
30	9	369	5.32	5.47	5.63	5.79	5.95	6.11	6.28	6.44	6.61	6.78	6.95	7.13	7.30	7.48	7.65	7.83	8.01	8.19	8.38	8.56
30	8	368	5.32	5.48	5.63	5.79	5.95	6.12	6.28	6.45	6.62	6.79	6.96	7.13	7.31	7.48	7.66	7.84	8.02	8.20	8.38	8.57
30	7	367	5.33	5.48	5.64	5.80	5.96	6.12	6.29	6.45	6.62	6.79	6.96	7.14	7.31	7.49	7.66	7.84	8.02	8.20	8.39	8.57
30	6	366	5.34	5.49	5.65	5.80	5.97	6.13	6.29	6.46	6.63	6.80	6.97	7.14	7.32	7.49	7.67	7.85	8.03	8.21	8.39	8.57
30	5	365	5.34	5.50	5.65	5.81	5.97	6.13	6.30	6.46	6.63	6.80	6.97	7.15	7.32	7.49	7.67	7.85	8.03	8.21	8.39	8.58
30	4	364	5.35	5.50	5.66	5.82	5.98	6.14	6.30	6.47	6.64	6.81	6.98	7.15	7.33	7.50	7.68	7.85	8.03	8.22	8.40	8.58
30	3	363	5.35	5.51	5.66	5.82	5.98	6.14	6.31	6.47	6.64	6.81	6.98	7.16	7.33	7.50	7.68	7.86	8.04	8.22	8.40	8.58
30	2	362	5.36	5.51	5.67	5.83	5.99	6.15	6.31	6.48	6.65	6.82	6.99	7.16	7.33	7.51	7.68	7.86	8.04	8.22	8.41	8.59
30	1	361	5.37	5.52	5.68	5.83	5.99	6.16	6.32	6.49	6.65	6.82	6.99	7.16	7.34	7.51	7.69	7.87	8.05	8.23	8.41	8.59
30	0	360	5.37	5.53	5.68	5.84	6.00	6.16	6.33	6.49	6.66	6.83	7.00	7.17	7.34	7.52	7.69	7.87	8.05	8.23	8.41	8.60
29	11	359	5.38	5.53	5.69	5.85	6.01	6.17	6.33	6.50	6.66	6.83	7.00	7.17	7.35	7.52	7.70	7.88	8.06	8.24	8.42	8.60
29	10	358	5.39	5.54	5.70	5.85	6.01	6.17	6.34	6.50	6.67	6.84	7.01	7.18	7.35	7.53	7.70	7.88	8.06	8.24	8.42	8.60
29	9	357	5.39	5.55	5.70	5.86	6.02	6.18	6.34	6.51	6.67	6.84	7.01	7.18	7.36	7.53	7.71	7.89	8.06	8.24	8.43	8.61
29	8	356	5.40	5.55	5.71	5.87	6.02	6.19	6.35	6.51	6.68	6.85	7.02	7.19	7.36	7.54	7.71	7.89	8.07	8.25	8.43	8.61
29	7	355	5.41	5.56	5.71	5.87	6.03	6.19	6.36	6.52	6.69	6.85	7.02	7.19	7.37	7.54	7.72	7.90	8.07	8.25	8.44	8.62
29	6	354	5.41	5.57	5.72	5.88	6.04	6.20	6.37	6.53	6.69	6.86	7.03	7.20	7.37	7.55	7.72	7.90	8.08	8.26	8.44	8.62
29	5	353	5.42	5.57	5.73	5.88	6.04	6.20	6.37	6.53	6.70	6.86	7.03	7.21	7.38	7.55	7.73	7.90	8.08	8.26	8.44	8.63
29	4	352	5.43	5.58	5.73	5.89	6.05	6.21	6.38	6.54	6.70	6.87	7.04	7.21	7.38	7.56	7.73	7.91	8.09	8.27	8.45	8.63
29	3	351	5.43	5.59	5.74	5.90	6.06	6.22	6.38	6.54	6.71	6.88	7.05	7.22	7.39	7.56	7.74	7.91	8.09	8.27	8.45	8.63
29	2	350	5.44	5.59	5.75	5.90	6.06	6.22	6.39	6.55	6.71	6.88	7.05	7.22	7.39	7.57	7.74	7.92	8.10	8.28	8.46	8.64
29	1	349	5.45	5.60	5.75	5.91	6.07	6.23	6.39	6.55	6.72	6.89	7.06	7.23	7.40	7.57	7.75	7.92	8.10	8.28	8.46	8.64
29	0	348	5.45	5.61	5.76	5.92	6.08	6.24	6.40	6.56	6.73	6.89	7.06	7.23	7.40	7.58	7.75	7.93	8.11	8.29	8.47	8.65
28	11	347	5.46	5.61	5.77	5.92	6.08	6.24	6.40	6.57	6.73	6.90	7.07	7.24	7.41	7.58	7.76	7.93	8.11	8.29	8.47	8.65
28	10	346	5.47	5.62	5.77	5.93	6.09	6.25	6.41	6.57	6.74	6.91	7.07	7.24	7.42	7.59	7.76	7.94	8.12	8.30	8.47	8.66
28	9	345	5.47	5.63	5.78	5.94	6.09	6.25	6.42	6.58	6.74	6.91	7.08	7.25	7.42	7.59	7.77	7.94	8.12	8.30	8.48	8.66
28	8	344	5.48	5.63	5.79	5.94	6.10	6.26	6.42	6.59	6.75	6.92	7.09	7.26	7.43	7.60	7.77	7.95	8.13	8.31	8.48	8.67
28	7	343	5.49	5.64	5.79	5.95	6.11	6.27	6.43	6.59	6.76	6.92	7.09	7.26	7.43	7.60	7.78	7.95	8.13	8.31	8.49	8.67
28	6	342	5.50	5.65	5.80	5.96	6.11	6.27	6.44	6.60	6.76	6.93	7.10	7.27	7.44	7.61	7.78	7.96	8.14	8.31	8.49	8.67

AMORTIZATION TABLES (Continued)

MONTHLY INSTALLMENT PER THOUSAND DOLLARS INCLUDING INTEREST AT—

Years	Months	No. of Payments	5%	5¼%	5½%	5¾%	6%	6¼%	6½%	6¾%	7%	7¼%	7½%	7¾%	8%	8¼%	8½%	8¾%	9%	9¼%	9½%	9¾%
28	5	341	5.50	5.66	5.81	5.96	6.12	6.28	6.44	6.60	6.77	6.94	7.10	7.27	7.44	7.62	7.79	7.96	8.14	8.32	8.50	8.68
28	4	340	5.51	5.66	5.82	5.97	6.13	6.29	6.45	6.61	6.78	6.94	7.11	7.28	7.45	7.62	7.80	7.97	8.15	8.32	8.50	8.68
28	3	339	5.52	5.67	5.82	5.98	6.14	6.29	6.45	6.62	6.78	6.95	7.12	7.28	7.45	7.63	7.80	7.98	8.15	8.33	8.51	8.69
28	2	338	5.53	5.68	5.83	5.99	6.14	6.30	6.46	6.62	6.79	6.95	7.12	7.29	7.46	7.63	7.81	7.98	8.16	8.33	8.51	8.69
28	1	337	5.53	5.68	5.84	5.99	6.15	6.31	6.47	6.63	6.79	6.96	7.13	7.30	7.47	7.64	7.81	7.99	8.16	8.34	8.52	8.70
28	0	336	5.54	5.69	5.84	6.00	6.16	6.31	6.48	6.64	6.80	6.97	7.13	7.30	7.47	7.64	7.82	7.99	8.17	8.35	8.52	8.70
27	11	335	5.55	5.70	5.85	6.01	6.16	6.32	6.48	6.64	6.81	6.97	7.14	7.31	7.48	7.65	7.82	8.00	8.17	8.35	8.53	8.71
27	10	334	5.56	5.71	5.86	6.01	6.17	6.33	6.49	6.65	6.81	6.98	7.15	7.31	7.48	7.66	7.83	8.00	8.18	8.36	8.53	8.71
27	9	333	5.56	5.71	5.87	6.02	6.18	6.34	6.50	6.66	6.82	6.99	7.15	7.32	7.49	7.66	7.83	8.01	8.18	8.36	8.54	8.72
27	8	332	5.57	5.72	5.87	6.03	6.18	6.34	6.50	6.66	6.83	6.99	7.16	7.33	7.50	7.67	7.84	8.01	8.19	8.37	8.54	8.72
27	7	331	5.58	5.73	5.88	6.04	6.19	6.35	6.51	6.67	6.83	7.00	7.17	7.33	7.50	7.67	7.85	8.02	8.20	8.37	8.55	8.73
27	6	330	5.59	5.74	5.89	6.04	6.20	6.36	6.52	6.68	6.84	7.01	7.17	7.34	7.51	7.68	7.85	8.03	8.20	8.38	8.56	8.73
27	5	329	5.59	5.75	5.90	6.05	6.21	6.36	6.52	6.69	6.85	7.01	7.18	7.35	7.52	7.69	7.86	8.03	8.21	8.38	8.56	8.73
27	4	328	5.60	5.75	5.90	6.06	6.21	6.37	6.53	6.69	6.85	7.02	7.19	7.35	7.52	7.69	7.86	8.04	8.21	8.39	8.57	8.74
27	3	327	5.61	5.76	5.91	6.07	6.22	6.38	6.54	6.70	6.86	7.03	7.19	7.36	7.53	7.70	7.87	8.04	8.22	8.39	8.57	8.75
27	2	326	5.62	5.77	5.92	6.07	6.23	6.39	6.55	6.71	6.87	7.03	7.20	7.37	7.53	7.71	7.88	8.05	8.22	8.40	8.58	8.76
27	1	325	5.63	5.78	5.93	6.08	6.24	6.39	6.55	6.71	6.88	7.04	7.21	7.37	7.54	7.71	7.88	8.06	8.23	8.41	8.58	8.76
27	0	324	5.64	5.78	5.94	6.09	6.24	6.40	6.56	6.72	6.88	7.05	7.21	7.38	7.55	7.72	7.89	8.06	8.24	8.41	8.59	8.77
26	11	323	5.64	5.79	5.94	6.10	6.25	6.41	6.57	6.73	6.89	7.05	7.22	7.39	7.55	7.72	7.90	8.07	8.24	8.42	8.59	8.77
26	10	322	5.65	5.80	5.95	6.11	6.26	6.42	6.58	6.74	6.90	7.06	7.23	7.39	7.56	7.73	7.90	8.07	8.25	8.42	8.60	8.78
26	9	321	5.66	5.81	5.96	6.11	6.27	6.42	6.58	6.74	6.90	7.07	7.23	7.40	7.57	7.74	7.91	8.08	8.25	8.43	8.61	8.78
26	8	320	5.67	5.82	5.97	6.12	6.28	6.43	6.59	6.75	6.91	7.07	7.24	7.41	7.57	7.74	7.91	8.09	8.26	8.44	8.61	8.79
26	7	319	5.68	5.83	5.98	6.13	6.28	6.44	6.60	6.76	6.92	7.08	7.25	7.41	7.58	7.75	7.92	8.09	8.27	8.44	8.62	8.80
26	6	318	5.69	5.83	5.99	6.14	6.29	6.45	6.61	6.77	6.93	7.09	7.25	7.42	7.59	7.75	7.93	8.10	8.27	8.45	8.62	8.80
26	5	317	5.69	5.84	5.99	6.15	6.30	6.46	6.61	6.77	6.93	7.10	7.26	7.43	7.60	7.76	7.93	8.11	8.28	8.45	8.63	8.81
26	4	316	5.70	5.85	6.00	6.15	6.31	6.46	6.62	6.78	6.94	7.10	7.27	7.43	7.60	7.77	7.94	8.11	8.29	8.46	8.64	8.81
26	3	315	5.71	5.86	6.01	6.16	6.32	6.47	6.63	6.79	6.95	7.11	7.28	7.44	7.61	7.78	7.95	8.12	8.29	8.47	8.64	8.82
26	2	314	5.72	5.87	6.02	6.17	6.32	6.48	6.64	6.80	6.96	7.12	7.28	7.45	7.62	7.79	7.95	8.13	8.30	8.47	8.65	8.82
26	1	313	5.73	5.88	6.03	6.18	6.33	6.49	6.65	6.80	6.97	7.13	7.29	7.46	7.62	7.79	7.96	8.13	8.31	8.48	8.65	8.83
26	0	312	5.74	5.89	6.04	6.19	6.34	6.50	6.65	6.81	6.97	7.14	7.30	7.46	7.63	7.80	7.97	8.14	8.31	8.49	8.66	8.84
25	11	311	5.75	5.90	6.05	6.20	6.35	6.51	6.66	6.82	6.98	7.14	7.31	7.47	7.64	7.81	7.98	8.15	8.32	8.49	8.67	8.84

Yr	Mo	No																				
25	10	310	5.76	5.90	6.05	6.21	6.36	6.51	6.67	6.83	6.99	7.15	7.31	7.48	7.65	7.81	7.98	8.15	8.33	8.50	8.67	8.85
25	9	309	5.77	5.91	6.06	6.21	6.37	6.52	6.68	6.84	7.00	7.16	7.32	7.49	7.65	7.82	7.99	8.16	8.33	8.51	8.68	8.86
25	8	308	5.77	5.92	6.07	6.22	6.38	6.53	6.69	6.85	7.01	7.17	7.33	7.49	7.66	7.83	8.00	8.17	8.34	8.51	8.69	8.86
25	7	307	5.78	5.93	6.08	6.23	6.38	6.54	6.70	6.86	7.01	7.17	7.34	7.50	7.67	7.84	8.00	8.17	8.35	8.52	8.69	8.87
25	6	306	5.79	5.94	6.09	6.24	6.39	6.55	6.71	6.87	7.02	7.18	7.35	7.51	7.68	7.84	8.01	8.18	8.35	8.53	8.70	8.88
25	5	305	5.80	5.95	6.10	6.25	6.40	6.56	6.72	6.88	7.03	7.19	7.35	7.52	7.68	7.85	8.02	8.19	8.36	8.53	8.71	8.88
25	4	304	5.81	5.96	6.11	6.26	6.41	6.57	6.73	6.89	7.04	7.20	7.36	7.53	7.69	7.86	8.03	8.20	8.37	8.54	8.71	8.89
25	3	303	5.82	5.97	6.12	6.27	6.42	6.57	6.74	6.90	7.05	7.21	7.37	7.53	7.70	7.87	8.03	8.20	8.37	8.55	8.72	8.90
25	2	302	5.83	5.98	6.13	6.28	6.43	6.58	6.74	6.90	7.06	7.22	7.38	7.54	7.71	7.87	8.04	8.21	8.38	8.55	8.73	8.90
25	1	301	5.84	5.99	6.14	6.29	6.44	6.59	6.75	6.91	7.06	7.22	7.39	7.55	7.72	7.88	8.05	8.22	8.39	8.56	8.73	8.91
25	0	300	5.85	6.00	6.15	6.30	6.45	6.60	6.76	6.91	7.07	7.23	7.39	7.56	7.72	7.89	8.06	8.23	8.40	8.57	8.74	8.92
24	11	299	5.86	6.01	6.16	6.31	6.46	6.61	6.77	6.92	7.08	7.24	7.40	7.57	7.73	7.90	8.07	8.23	8.40	8.58	8.75	8.92
24	10	298	5.87	6.02	6.17	6.32	6.47	6.62	6.78	6.93	7.09	7.25	7.41	7.57	7.74	7.91	8.07	8.24	8.41	8.58	8.76	8.93
24	9	297	5.88	6.03	6.17	6.32	6.48	6.63	6.78	6.94	7.10	7.26	7.42	7.58	7.75	7.91	8.08	8.25	8.42	8.59	8.76	8.94
24	8	296	5.89	6.04	6.18	6.33	6.49	6.64	6.79	6.95	7.11	7.27	7.43	7.59	7.76	7.92	8.09	8.26	8.43	8.60	8.77	8.94
24	7	295	5.90	6.05	6.19	6.34	6.50	6.65	6.80	6.96	7.12	7.28	7.44	7.60	7.76	7.93	8.10	8.27	8.44	8.61	8.78	8.95
24	6	294	5.91	6.06	6.20	6.35	6.50	6.66	6.81	6.97	7.13	7.29	7.45	7.61	7.77	7.94	8.11	8.27	8.44	8.61	8.79	8.96
24	5	293	5.92	6.07	6.21	6.36	6.51	6.67	6.82	6.98	7.14	7.29	7.46	7.62	7.78	7.95	8.11	8.28	8.45	8.62	8.79	8.97
24	4	292	5.93	6.08	6.22	6.37	6.52	6.68	6.83	6.99	7.14	7.30	7.46	7.63	7.79	7.96	8.12	8.29	8.46	8.63	8.80	8.97
24	3	291	5.94	6.09	6.23	6.38	6.53	6.69	6.84	7.00	7.15	7.31	7.47	7.64	7.80	7.96	8.13	8.30	8.47	8.64	8.81	8.98
24	2	290	5.95	6.10	6.25	6.39	6.54	6.70	6.85	7.01	7.16	7.32	7.48	7.64	7.81	7.97	8.14	8.31	8.48	8.65	8.82	8.99
24	1	289	5.96	6.11	6.26	6.40	6.55	6.71	6.86	7.02	7.17	7.33	7.49	7.65	7.82	7.98	8.15	8.31	8.48	8.65	8.82	9.00
24	0	288	5.97	6.12	6.27	6.41	6.56	6.72	6.87	7.03	7.18	7.34	7.50	7.66	7.83	7.99	8.16	8.32	8.49	8.66	8.83	9.01
23	11	287	5.98	6.13	6.28	6.42	6.58	6.73	6.88	7.04	7.19	7.35	7.51	7.67	7.83	8.00	8.16	8.33	8.50	8.67	8.84	9.01
23	10	286	6.00	6.14	6.29	6.44	6.59	6.74	6.89	7.05	7.20	7.36	7.52	7.68	7.84	8.01	8.17	8.34	8.51	8.68	8.85	9.02
23	9	285	6.01	6.15	6.30	6.45	6.60	6.75	6.90	7.06	7.21	7.37	7.53	7.69	7.85	8.02	8.18	8.35	8.52	8.69	8.86	9.03
23	8	284	6.02	6.16	6.31	6.46	6.61	6.76	6.91	7.07	7.22	7.38	7.54	7.70	7.86	8.03	8.19	8.36	8.53	8.69	8.87	9.04
23	7	283	6.03	6.17	6.32	6.47	6.62	6.77	6.92	7.08	7.23	7.39	7.55	7.71	7.87	8.04	8.20	8.37	8.53	8.70	8.87	9.05
23	6	282	6.04	6.18	6.33	6.48	6.63	6.78	6.93	7.09	7.24	7.40	7.56	7.72	7.88	8.04	8.21	8.38	8.54	8.71	8.88	9.05
23	5	281	6.05	6.20	6.34	6.49	6.64	6.79	6.94	7.10	7.25	7.41	7.57	7.73	7.89	8.05	8.22	8.38	8.55	8.72	8.89	9.06
23	4	280	6.06	6.21	6.35	6.50	6.65	6.80	6.95	7.11	7.26	7.42	7.58	7.74	7.90	8.06	8.23	8.39	8.56	8.73	8.90	9.07
23	3	279	6.07	6.22	6.36	6.51	6.66	6.81	6.96	7.12	7.27	7.43	7.59	7.75	7.91	8.07	8.24	8.40	8.57	8.74	8.91	9.08
23	2	278	6.09	6.23	6.37	6.52	6.67	6.82	6.97	7.13	7.28	7.44	7.60	7.76	7.92	8.08	8.25	8.41	8.58	8.75	8.92	9.09
23	1	277	6.10	6.24	6.39	6.53	6.68	6.83	6.98	7.14	7.29	7.45	7.61	7.77	7.93	8.09	8.26	8.42	8.59	8.76	8.93	9.10
23	0	276	6.11	6.25	6.40	6.54	6.69	6.84	7.00	7.15	7.30	7.46	7.62	7.78	7.94	8.10	8.27	8.43	8.60	8.77	8.93	9.11
22	11	275	6.12	6.26	6.41	6.56	6.70	6.85	7.01	7.16	7.31	7.47	7.63	7.79	7.95	8.11	8.28	8.44	8.61	8.77	8.94	9.11
22	10	274	6.13	6.28	6.42	6.57	6.72	6.87	7.02	7.17	7.33	7.48	7.64	7.80	7.96	8.12	8.29	8.45	8.62	8.78	8.95	9.12
22	9	273	6.14	6.29	6.43	6.58	6.73	6.88	7.03	7.18	7.34	7.49	7.65	7.81	7.97	8.13	8.30	8.46	8.63	8.79	8.96	9.13

AMORTIZATION TABLES (Continued)

MONTHLY INSTALLMENT PER THOUSAND DOLLARS INCLUDING INTEREST AT—

Years	Months	No. of Payments	5%	5¼%	5½%	5¾%	6%	6¼%	6½%	6¾%	7%	7¼%	7½%	7¾%	8%	8¼%	8½%	8¾%	9%	9¼%	9½%	9¾%
22	8	272	6.16	6.30	6.44	6.59	6.74	6.89	7.04	7.19	7.35	7.50	7.66	7.82	7.98	8.14	8.31	8.47	8.61	8.80	8.97	9.14
22	7	271	6.17	6.31	6.46	6.60	6.75	6.90	7.05	7.20	7.36	7.51	7.67	7.83	7.99	8.15	8.32	8.48	8.65	8.81	8.98	9.15
22	6	270	6.18	6.32	6.47	6.62	6.76	6.91	7.06	7.22	7.37	7.53	7.68	7.84	8.00	8.16	8.33	8.49	8.66	8.82	8.99	9.16
22	5	269	6.19	6.34	6.48	6.63	6.79	6.97	7.07	7.23	7.38	7.54	7.69	7.85	8.01	8.17	8.34	8.50	8.67	8.83	9.00	9.17
22	4	268	6.21	6.35	6.49	6.64	6.79	6.94	7.09	7.24	7.39	7.55	7.70	7.86	8.02	8.18	8.35	8.51	8.68	8.84	9.01	9.18
22	3	267	6.22	6.36	6.51	6.65	6.80	6.95	7.10	7.25	7.40	7.56	7.72	7.87	8.03	8.19	8.36	8.52	8.65	8.85	9.02	9.19
22	2	266	6.23	6.37	6.52	6.66	6.81	6.96	7.11	7.26	7.42	7.57	7.73	7.89	8.04	8.21	8.37	8.53	8.70	8.86	9.03	9.20
22	1	265	6.24	6.39	6.53	6.68	6.82	6.97	7.12	7.27	7.43	7.58	7.74	7.90	8.06	8.22	8.38	8.54	8.71	8.87	9.04	9.21
22	0	264	6.26	6.40	6.54	6.69	6.84	6.98	7.13	7.29	7.44	7.59	7.75	7.91	8.07	8.23	8.39	8.55	8.72	8.88	9.05	9.22
21	11	263	6.27	6.41	6.56	6.70	6.85	7.00	7.15	7.30	7.45	7.61	7.76	7.92	8.08	8.24	8.40	8.56	8.73	8.89	9.06	9.23
21	10	262	6.28	6.43	6.57	6.71	6.86	7.01	7.16	7.31	7.46	7.62	7.77	7.93	8.09	8.25	8.41	8.57	8.74	8.90	9.07	9.24
21	9	261	6.30	6.44	6.58	6.73	6.87	7.02	7.17	7.32	7.48	7.63	7.79	7.94	8.10	8.26	8.42	8.58	8.75	8.91	9.08	9.25
21	8	260	6.31	6.45	6.60	6.74	6.89	7.03	7.18	7.34	7.49	7.64	7.80	7.95	8.11	8.27	8.43	8.60	8.76	8.92	9.09	9.26
21	7	259	6.32	6.47	6.61	6.75	6.90	7.05	7.20	7.35	7.50	7.65	7.81	7.97	8.12	8.28	8.44	8.61	8.77	8.94	9.10	9.27
21	6	258	6.34	6.48	6.62	6.77	6.91	7.06	7.21	7.36	7.51	7.67	7.82	7.98	8.14	8.30	8.46	8.62	8.78	8.95	9.11	9.28
21	5	257	6.35	6.49	6.64	6.78	6.93	7.07	7.22	7.37	7.53	7.68	7.83	7.99	8.15	8.31	8.47	8.63	8.79	8.96	9.12	9.29
21	4	256	6.37	6.51	6.65	6.79	6.94	7.09	7.24	7.39	7.54	7.69	7.85	8.00	8.16	8.32	8.48	8.64	8.80	8.97	9.13	9.30
21	3	255	6.38	6.52	6.66	6.81	6.95	7.10	7.25	7.40	7.55	7.70	7.86	8.01	8.17	8.33	8.49	8.65	8.82	8.98	9.15	9.31
21	2	254	6.39	6.53	6.68	6.82	6.97	7.11	7.26	7.41	7.56	7.72	7.87	8.03	8.18	8.34	8.50	8.66	8.83	8.99	9.16	9.32
21	1	253	641	6.55	6.69	6.83	6.98	7.13	7.28	7.43	7.58	7.73	7.88	8.04	8.20	8.36	8.52	8.68	8.84	9.00	9.17	9.33
21	0	252	6.42	6.56	6.70	6.85	6.99	7.14	7.29	7.44	7.59	7.74	7.90	8.05	8.21	8.37	8.53	8.69	8.85	9.01	9.18	9.35
20	11	251	6.44	6.58	6.72	6.86	7.01	7.15	7.30	7.45	7.60	7.76	7.91	8.07	8.22	8.38	8.54	8.70	8.86	9.03	9.19	9.36
20	10	250	6.45	6.59	6.73	6.88	7.02	7.17	7.32	7.47	7.62	7.77	7.92	8.08	8.23	8.39	8.55	8.71	8.87	9.04	9.20	9.37
20	9	249	6.47	6.61	6.75	6.89	7.04	7.18	7.33	7.48	7.63	7.78	7.94	8.09	8.25	8.41	8.56	8.73	8.89	9.05	9.21	9.38
20	8	248	6.48	6.62	6.76	6.91	7.05	7.20	7.34	7.49	7.64	7.80	7.95	8.10	8.26	8.42	8.58	8.74	8.90	9.06	9.23	9.39
20	7	247	6.50	6.64	6.78	6.92	7.06	7.21	7.36	7.51	7.66	7.81	7.96	8.12	8.27	8.43	8.59	8.75	8.91	9.07	9.24	9.40
20	6	246	6.51	6.65	6.79	6.93	7.08	7.22	7.37	7.52	7.67	7.82	7.98	8.13	8.29	8.44	8.60	8.76	8.92	9.09	9.25	9.42
20	5	245	6.53	6.67	6.81	6.95	7.09	7.24	7.39	7.54	7.69	7.84	7.99	8.14	8.30	8.46	8.62	8.78	8.94	9.10	9.26	9.43
20	4	244	6.54	6.68	6.82	6.96	7.11	7.25	7.40	7.55	7.70	7.85	8.00	8.16	8.31	8.47	8.63	8.79	8.95	9.11	9.28	9.44
20	3	243	6.56	6.70	6.84	6.98	7.12	7.27	7.42	7.56	7.71	7.87	8.02	8.17	8.33	8.48	8.64	8.80	8.96	9.12	9.29	9.45
20	2	242	6.57	6.71	6.85	6.99	7.14	7.28	7.43	7.58	7.73	7.88	8.03	8.19	8.34	8.50	8.66	8.82	8.98	9.14	9.30	9.46
20	1	241	6.59	6.73	6.87	7.01	7.15	7.30	7.45	7.59	7.74	7.89	8.05	8.20	8.36	8.51	8.67	8.83	8.99	9.15	9.31	9.48

Yrs	Mos	No.																				
20	0	240	6.60	6.74	6.88	7.03	7.17	7.31	7.46	7.61	7.76	7.91	8.06	8.21	8.37	8.53	8.68	8.84	9.00	9.16	9.33	9.49
19	11	239	6.62	6.76	6.90	7.04	7.18	7.33	7.48	7.62	7.77	7.92	8.08	8.23	8.38	8.54	8.70	8.86	9.02	9.18	9.34	9.50
19	10	238	6.64	6.78	6.92	7.06	7.20	7.35	7.49	7.64	7.79	7.94	8.09	8.24	8.40	8.55	8.71	8.87	9.03	9.19	9.35	9.52
19	9	237	6.65	6.79	6.93	7.07	7.22	7.36	7.51	7.65	7.80	7.95	8.11	8.26	8.41	8.57	8.73	8.88	9.04	9.20	9.37	9.53
19	8	236	6.67	6.81	6.95	7.09	7.23	7.38	7.52	7.67	7.82	7.97	8.12	8.27	8.43	8.58	8.74	8.90	9.06	9.22	9.38	9.54
19	7	235	6.69	6.82	6.96	7.11	7.25	7.39	7.54	7.69	7.83	7.98	8.14	8.29	8.44	8.60	8.75	8.91	9.07	9.23	9.39	9.56
19	6	234	6.70	6.84	6.98	7.12	7.26	7.41	7.55	7.70	7.85	8.00	8.15	8.30	8.46	8.61	8.77	8.93	9.09	9.25	9.41	9.57
19	5	233	6.72	6.86	7.00	7.14	7.28	7.43	7.57	7.72	7.87	8.02	8.17	8.32	8.47	8.63	8.78	8.94	9.10	9.26	9.42	9.58
19	4	232	6.74	6.88	7.01	7.16	7.30	7.44	7.59	7.73	7.88	8.03	8.18	8.33	8.49	8.64	8.80	8.96	9.11	9.27	9.44	9.60
19	3	231	6.75	6.89	7.03	7.17	7.31	7.46	7.60	7.75	7.90	8.05	8.20	8.35	8.50	8.66	8.81	8.97	9.13	9.29	9.45	9.61
19	2	230	6.77	6.91	7.05	7.19	7.33	7.47	7.62	7.77	7.91	8.06	8.21	8.37	8.52	8.67	8.83	8.99	9.14	9.30	9.46	9.63
19	1	229	6.79	6.93	7.07	7.21	7.35	7.49	7.64	7.78	7.93	8.08	8.23	8.38	8.53	8.69	8.84	9.00	9.16	9.32	9.48	9.64
19	0	228	6.81	6.95	7.08	7.22	7.37	7.51	7.65	7.80	7.95	8.10	8.25	8.40	8.55	8.70	8.86	9.02	9.17	9.33	9.49	9.65
18	11	227	6.83	6.96	7.10	7.24	7.38	7.53	7.67	7.82	7.96	8.11	8.26	8.41	8.57	8.72	8.88	9.03	9.19	9.35	9.51	9.67
18	10	226	6.84	6.98	7.12	7.26	7.40	7.54	7.69	7.83	7.98	8.13	8.28	8.43	8.58	8.74	8.89	9.05	9.20	9.36	9.52	9.68
18	9	225	6.86	7.00	7.14	7.28	7.42	7.56	7.71	7.85	8.00	8.15	8.30	8.45	8.60	8.75	8.91	9.06	9.22	9.38	9.54	9.70
18	8	224	6.88	7.02	7.16	7.30	7.44	7.58	7.72	7.87	8.02	8.16	8.31	8.46	8.62	8.77	8.92	9.08	9.24	9.39	9.55	9.71
18	7	223	6.90	7.04	7.17	7.31	7.45	7.60	7.74	7.89	8.03	8.18	8.33	8.48	8.63	8.79	8.94	9.10	9.25	9.41	9.57	9.73
18	6	222	6.92	7.05	7.19	7.33	7.47	7.62	7.76	7.90	8.05	8.20	8.35	8.50	8.65	8.80	8.96	9.11	9.27	9.43	9.59	9.75
18	5	221	6.94	7.07	7.21	7.35	7.49	7.63	7.78	7.92	8.07	8.22	8.36	8.51	8.67	8.82	8.97	9.13	9.28	9.44	9.60	9.76
18	4	220	6.96	7.09	7.23	7.37	7.51	7.65	7.80	7.94	8.09	8.23	8.38	8.53	8.68	8.84	8.99	9.15	9.30	9.46	9.62	9.78
18	3	219	6.98	7.11	7.25	7.39	7.53	7.67	7.81	7.96	8.10	8.25	8.40	8.55	8.70	8.85	9.01	9.16	9.32	9.48	9.63	9.79
18	2	218	7.00	7.13	7.27	7.41	7.55	7.69	7.83	7.98	8.12	8.27	8.42	8.57	8.72	8.87	9.02	9.18	9.34	9.49	9.65	9.81
18	1	217	7.02	7.15	7.29	7.43	7.57	7.71	7.85	8.00	8.14	8.29	8.44	8.59	8.74	8.89	9.04	9.20	9.35	9.51	9.67	9.83
18	0	216	7.04	7.17	7.31	7.45	7.59	7.73	7.87	8.01	8.16	8.31	8.45	8.60	8.75	8.91	9.06	9.21	9.37	9.53	9.68	9.84
17	11	215	7.06	7.19	7.33	7.47	7.61	7.75	7.89	8.03	8.18	8.33	8.47	8.62	8.77	8.92	9.08	9.23	9.39	9.54	9.70	9.86
17	10	214	7.08	7.21	7.35	7.49	7.63	7.77	7.91	8.05	8.20	8.34	8.49	8.64	8.79	8.94	9.10	9.25	9.40	9.56	9.72	9.88
17	9	213	7.10	7.23	7.37	7.51	7.65	7.79	7.93	8.07	8.22	8.36	8.51	8.66	8.81	8.96	9.11	9.27	9.42	9.58	9.74	9.89
17	8	212	7.12	7.25	7.39	7.53	7.67	7.81	7.95	8.09	8.24	8.38	8.53	8.68	8.83	8.98	9.13	9.29	9.44	9.60	9.75	9.91
17	7	211	7.14	7.27	7.41	7.55	7.69	7.83	7.97	8.11	8.26	8.40	8.55	8.70	8.85	9.00	9.15	9.30	9.46	9.61	9.77	9.93
17	6	210	7.16	7.29	7.43	7.57	7.71	7.85	7.99	8.13	8.28	8.42	8.57	8.72	8.87	9.02	9.17	9.32	9.48	9.63	9.79	9.95
17	5	209	7.18	7.32	7.45	7.59	7.73	7.87	8.01	8.15	8.30	8.44	8.59	8.74	8.89	9.04	9.19	9.34	9.50	9.65	9.81	9.97
17	4	208	7.20	7.34	7.47	7.61	7.75	7.89	8.03	8.17	8.32	8.46	8.61	8.76	8.91	9.06	9.21	9.36	9.52	9.67	9.83	9.98
17	3	207	7.22	7.36	7.49	7.63	7.77	7.91	8.05	8.19	8.34	8.48	8.63	8.78	8.93	9.08	9.23	9.38	9.53	9.69	9.85	10.00
17	2	206	7.25	7.38	7.52	7.65	7.79	7.93	8.07	8.22	8.36	8.50	8.65	8.80	8.95	9.10	9.25	9.40	9.55	9.71	9.86	10.02
17	1	205	7.27	7.40	7.54	7.68	7.81	7.95	8.09	8.24	8.38	8.53	8.67	8.82	8.97	9.12	9.27	9.42	9.57	9.73	9.88	10.04
17	0	204	7.29	7.43	7.56	7.70	7.84	7.98	8.12	8.26	8.40	8.55	8.69	8.84	8.99	9.14	9.29	9.44	9.59	9.75	9.90	10.06
16	11	203	7.31	7.45	7.58	7.72	7.86	8.00	8.14	8.28	8.42	8.57	8.71	8.86	9.01	9.16	9.31	9.46	9.61	9.77	9.92	10.08

AMORTIZATION TABLES (Continued)

MONTHLY INSTALLMENT PER THOUSAND DOLLARS INCLUDING INTEREST AT—

Term of Mortgage Years	Months	No. of Payments	5%	5¼%	5½%	5¾%	6%	6¼%	6½%	6¾%	7%	7¼%	7½%	7¾%	8%	8¼%	8½%	8¾%	9%	9¼%	9½%	9¾%
16	10	202	7.34	7.47	7.61	7.74	7.88	8.02	8.16	8.30	8.45	8.59	8.73	8.88	9.03	9.18	9.33	9.48	9.63	9.79	9.94	10.10
16	9	201	7.36	7.49	7.63	7.77	7.90	8.04	8.18	8.32	8.47	8.61	8.76	8.90	9.05	9.20	9.35	9.50	9.65	9.81	9.96	10.12
16	8	200	7.38	7.52	7.65	7.79	7.93	8.07	8.21	8.35	8.49	8.63	8.78	8.92	9.07	9.22	9.37	9.52	9.67	9.83	9.98	10.14
16	7	199	7.41	7.54	7.68	7.81	7.95	8.09	8.23	8.37	8.51	8.66	8.80	8.95	9.09	9.24	9.39	9.54	9.70	9.85	10.00	10.16
16	6	198	7.43	7.57	7.70	7.84	7.97	8.11	8.25	8.39	8.53	8.68	8.82	8.97	9.12	9.26	9.41	9.57	9.72	9.87	10.02	10.18
16	5	197	7.46	7.59	7.72	7.86	8.00	8.14	8.27	8.42	8.56	8.70	8.85	8.99	9.14	9.29	9.44	9.59	9.74	9.89	10.05	10.20
16	4	196	7.48	7.61	7.75	7.88	8.02	8.16	8.30	8.44	8.58	8.72	8.87	9.01	9.16	9.31	9.46	9.61	9.76	9.91	10.07	10.22
16	3	195	7.51	7.64	7.77	7.91	8.05	8.18	8.32	8.46	8.60	8.75	8.89	9.04	9.18	9.33	9.48	9.63	9.78	9.93	10.09	10.24
16	2	194	7.53	7.66	7.80	7.93	8.07	8.21	8.35	8.49	8.63	8.77	8.92	9.06	9.21	9.35	9.50	9.65	9.80	9.96	10.11	10.26
16	1	193	7.56	7.69	7.82	7.96	8.09	8.23	8.37	8.51	8.65	8.80	8.94	9.08	9.23	9.38	9.53	9.68	9.83	9.98	10.13	10.29
16	0	192	7.58	7.71	7.85	7.98	8.12	8.26	8.40	8.54	8.68	8.82	8.96	9.11	9.25	9.40	9.55	9.70	9.85	10.00	10.15	10.31
15	11	191	7.61	7.74	7.87	8.01	8.14	8.28	8.42	8.56	8.70	8.84	8.99	9.13	9.28	9.43	9.57	9.72	9.87	10.02	10.18	10.33
15	10	190	7.63	7.77	7.90	8.03	8.17	8.31	8.45	8.59	8.73	8.87	9.01	9.16	9.30	9.45	9.60	9.75	9.90	10.05	10.20	10.35
15	9	189	7.66	7.79	7.93	8.06	8.20	8.33	8.47	8.61	8.75	8.89	9.04	9.18	9.33	9.47	9.62	9.77	9.92	10.07	10.22	10.38
15	8	188	7.69	7.82	7.95	8.09	8.22	8.36	8.50	8.64	8.78	8.92	9.06	9.21	9.35	9.50	9.65	9.79	9.94	10.10	10.25	10.40
15	7	187	7.71	7.85	7.98	8.11	8.25	8.39	8.52	8.66	8.80	8.95	9.09	9.23	9.38	9.52	9.67	9.82	9.97	10.12	10.27	10.42
15	6	186	7.74	7.87	8.01	8.14	8.28	8.41	8.55	8.69	8.83	8.97	9.11	9.26	9.40	9.55	9.70	9.84	9.99	10.14	10.30	10.45
15	5	185	7.77	7.90	8.03	8.17	8.30	8.44	8.58	8.72	8.86	9.00	9.14	9.28	9.43	9.57	9.72	9.87	10.02	10.17	10.32	10.47
15	4	184	7.80	7.93	8.06	8.20	8.33	8.47	8.60	8.74	8.88	9.02	9.17	9.31	9.45	9.60	9.75	9.89	10.04	10.19	10.34	10.50
15	3	183	7.83	7.96	8.09	8.22	8.36	8.49	8.63	8.77	8.91	9.05	9.19	9.34	9.48	9.63	9.77	9.92	10.07	10.22	10.37	10.52
15	2	182	7.85	7.99	8.12	8.25	8.39	8.52	8.66	8.80	8.94	9.08	9.22	9.36	9.51	9.65	9.80	9.95	10.09	10.24	10.40	10.55
15	1	181	7.88	8.01	8.15	8.28	8.41	8.55	8.69	8.83	8.97	9.11	9.25	9.39	9.53	9.68	9.83	9.97	10.12	10.27	10.42	10.57
15	0	180	7.91	8.04	8.18	8.31	8.44	8.58	8.72	8.85	8.99	9.13	9.28	9.42	9.56	9.71	9.85	10.00	10.15	10.30	10.45	10.60
14	11	179	7.94	8.07	8.21	8.34	8.47	8.61	8.74	8.88	9.02	9.16	9.30	9.45	9.59	9.73	9.88	10.03	10.17	10.32	10.47	10.62
14	10	178	7.97	8.10	8.24	8.37	8.50	8.64	8.77	8.91	9.05	9.19	9.33	9.47	9.62	9.76	9.91	10.05	10.20	10.35	10.50	10.65
14	9	177	8.00	8.13	8.27	8.40	8.53	8.67	8.80	8.94	9.08	9.22	9.36	9.50	9.65	9.79	9.94	10.08	10.23	10.38	10.53	10.68
14	8	176	8.03	8.16	8.30	8.43	8.56	8.70	8.83	8.97	9.11	9.25	9.39	9.53	9.67	9.82	9.96	10.11	10.26	10.41	10.56	10.71
14	7	175	8.06	8.20	8.33	8.46	8.59	8.73	8.86	9.00	9.14	9.28	9.42	9.56	9.70	9.85	9.99	10.14	10.29	10.43	10.58	10.73
14	6	174	8.10	8.23	8.36	8.49	8.62	8.76	8.89	9.03	9.17	9.31	9.45	9.59	9.73	9.88	10.02	10.17	10.31	10.46	10.61	10.76
14	5	173	8.13	8.26	8.39	8.52	8.65	8.79	8.93	9.06	9.20	9.34	9.48	9.62	9.76	9.91	10.05	10.20	10.34	10.49	10.64	10.79
14	4	172	8.16	8.29	8.42	8.55	8.69	8.82	8.96	9.09	9.23	9.37	9.51	9.65	9.79	9.94	10.08	10.23	10.37	10.52	10.67	10.82
14	3	171	8.19	8.32	8.45	8.59	8.72	8.85	8.99	9.12	9.26	9.40	9.54	9.68	9.82	9.97	10.11	10.26	10.40	10.55	10.70	10.85

Yr	Mo	Term																				
14	2	170	8.23	8.36	8.49	8.62	8.75	8.89	9.02	9.16	9.29	9.43	9.57	9.71	9.85	10.00	10.14	10.29	10.43	10.58	10.73	10.88
14	1	169	8.26	8.39	8.52	8.65	8.78	8.92	9.05	9.19	9.33	9.46	9.60	9.74	9.89	10.03	10.17	10.32	10.46	10.61	10.76	10.91
14	0	168	8.29	8.42	8.55	8.68	8.82	8.95	9.09	9.22	9.36	9.50	9.64	9.78	9.92	10.06	10.20	10.35	10.49	10.64	10.79	10.94
13	11	167	8.33	8.46	8.59	8.72	8.85	8.98	9.12	9.26	9.39	9.53	9.67	9.81	9.95	10.09	10.24	10.38	10.53	10.67	10.82	10.97
13	10	166	8.36	8.49	8.62	8.75	8.89	9.02	9.15	9.29	9.43	9.56	9.70	9.84	9.98	10.13	10.27	10.41	10.56	10.70	10.85	11.00
13	9	165	8.40	8.53	8.66	8.79	8.92	9.05	9.19	9.32	9.46	9.60	9.74	9.88	10.02	10.16	10.30	10.45	10.59	10.74	10.88	11.03
13	8	164	8.43	8.56	8.69	8.82	8.95	9.09	9.22	9.36	9.49	9.63	9.77	9.91	10.05	10.19	10.33	10.48	10.62	10.77	10.92	11.06
13	7	163	8.47	8.60	8.73	8.86	8.99	9.12	9.26	9.39	9.53	9.67	9.80	9.94	10.08	10.23	10.37	10.51	10.66	10.80	10.95	11.10
13	6	162	8.51	8.63	8.76	8.89	9.03	9.16	9.29	9.43	9.56	9.70	9.84	9.98	10.12	10.26	10.40	10.55	10.69	10.83	10.98	11.13
13	5	161	8.54	8.67	8.80	8.93	9.06	9.20	9.33	9.46	9.60	9.74	9.87	10.01	10.15	10.29	10.44	10.58	10.72	10.87	11.01	11.16
13	4	160	8.58	8.71	8.84	8.97	9.10	9.23	9.37	9.50	9.64	9.77	9.91	10.05	10.19	10.33	10.47	10.61	10.76	10.90	11.05	11.20
13	3	159	8.62	8.75	8.88	9.01	9.14	9.27	9.40	9.54	9.67	9.81	9.95	10.09	10.22	10.37	10.51	10.65	10.79	10.94	11.08	11.23
13	2	158	8.66	8.78	8.91	9.04	9.17	9.31	9.44	9.57	9.71	9.85	9.98	10.12	10.26	10.40	10.54	10.69	10.83	10.97	11.12	11.27
13	1	157	8.70	8.82	8.95	9.08	9.21	9.35	9.48	9.61	9.75	9.88	10.02	10.16	10.30	10.44	10.58	10.72	10.87	11.01	11.15	11.30
13	0	156	8.74	8.86	8.99	9.12	9.25	9.38	9.52	9.65	9.79	9.92	10.06	10.20	10.34	10.48	10.62	10.76	10.90	11.05	11.19	11.34
12	11	155	8.78	8.90	9.03	9.16	9.29	9.42	9.56	9.69	9.82	9.96	10.10	10.23	10.37	10.51	10.65	10.80	10.94	11.08	11.23	11.37
12	10	154	8.82	8.94	9.07	9.20	9.33	9.46	9.60	9.73	9.86	10.00	10.14	10.27	10.41	10.55	10.69	10.83	10.98	11.12	11.26	11.41
12	9	153	8.86	8.98	9.11	9.24	9.37	9.50	9.64	9.77	9.90	10.04	10.18	10.31	10.45	10.59	10.73	10.87	11.01	11.16	11.30	11.45
12	8	152	8.90	9.03	9.15	9.28	9.41	9.54	9.68	9.81	9.94	10.08	10.22	10.35	10.49	10.63	10.77	10.91	11.05	11.20	11.34	11.49
12	7	151	8.94	9.07	9.20	9.32	9.45	9.59	9.72	9.85	9.99	10.12	10.26	10.39	10.53	10.67	10.81	10.95	11.09	11.24	11.38	11.52
12	6	150	8.98	9.11	9.24	9.37	9.50	9.63	9.76	9.89	10.03	10.16	10.30	10.43	10.57	10.71	10.85	10.99	11.13	11.28	11.42	11.56
12	5	149	9.03	9.15	9.28	9.41	9.54	9.67	9.80	9.94	10.07	10.20	10.34	10.48	10.61	10.75	10.89	11.03	11.17	11.32	11.46	11.60
12	4	148	9.07	9.20	9.33	9.45	9.58	9.71	9.85	9.98	10.11	10.25	10.38	10.52	10.66	10.79	10.93	11.07	11.21	11.36	11.50	11.64
12	3	147	9.12	9.24	9.37	9.50	9.63	9.76	9.89	10.02	10.15	10.29	10.42	10.56	10.70	10.84	10.98	11.12	11.26	11.40	11.54	11.68
12	2	146	9.16	9.29	9.41	9.54	9.67	9.80	9.93	10.07	10.20	10.33	10.47	10.60	10.74	10.88	11.02	11.16	11.30	11.44	11.58	11.73
12	1	145	9.21	9.33	9.46	9.59	9.72	9.85	9.98	10.11	10.24	10.38	10.51	10.65	10.79	10.92	11.06	11.20	11.34	11.48	11.63	11.77
12	0	144	9.25	9.38	9.51	9.63	9.76	9.89	10.02	10.16	10.29	10.42	10.56	10.69	10.83	10.97	11.11	11.24	11.39	11.53	11.67	11.81
11	11	143	9.30	9.43	9.55	9.68	9.81	9.94	10.07	10.20	10.33	10.47	10.60	10.74	10.87	11.01	11.15	11.29	11.43	11.57	11.71	11.86
11	10	142	9.35	9.47	9.60	9.73	9.86	9.99	10.12	10.25	10.38	10.51	10.65	10.78	10.92	11.06	11.20	11.33	11.47	11.62	11.76	11.90
11	9	141	9.40	9.52	9.65	9.78	9.91	10.03	10.17	10.30	10.43	10.56	10.70	10.83	10.97	11.10	11.24	11.38	11.52	11.66	11.80	11.94
11	8	140	9.45	9.57	9.70	9.83	9.95	10.08	10.21	10.34	10.48	10.61	10.74	10.88	11.01	11.15	11.29	11.43	11.57	11.71	11.85	11.99
11	7	139	9.50	9.62	9.75	9.88	10.00	10.13	10.26	10.39	10.53	10.66	10.79	10.93	11.06	11.20	11.34	11.47	11.61	11.75	11.90	12.04
11	6	138	9.55	9.67	9.80	9.93	10.05	10.18	10.31	10.44	10.58	10.71	10.84	10.98	11.11	11.25	11.38	11.52	11.66	11.80	11.94	12.08
11	5	137	9.60	9.72	9.85	9.98	10.11	10.23	10.36	10.49	10.63	10.76	10.89	11.03	11.16	11.30	11.43	11.57	11.71	11.85	11.99	12.13
11	4	136	9.65	9.78	9.90	10.03	10.16	10.29	10.41	10.55	10.68	10.81	10.94	11.08	11.21	11.35	11.48	11.62	11.76	11.90	12.04	12.18
11	3	135	9.71	9.83	9.96	10.08	10.21	10.34	10.47	10.60	10.73	10.86	10.99	11.13	11.26	11.40	11.53	11.67	11.81	11.95	12.09	12.23
11	2	134	9.76	9.88	10.01	10.14	10.26	10.39	10.52	10.65	10.78	10.91	11.05	11.18	11.31	11.45	11.59	11.72	11.86	12.00	12.14	12.28
11	1	133	9.81	9.94	10.06	10.19	10.32	10.45	10.57	10.70	10.83	10.97	11.10	11.23	11.37	11.50	11.64	11.78	11.91	12.05	12.19	12.33

AMORTIZATION TABLES (Continued)

Term of Mortgage Years	Months	No. of Payments	MONTHLY INSTALLMENT PER THOUSAND DOLLARS INCLUDING INTEREST AT—																			
			5%	5¼%	5½%	5¾%	6%	6¼%	6½%	6¾%	7%	7¼%	7½%	7¾%	8%	8¼%	8½%	8¾%	9%	9¼%	9½%	9¾%
11	0	132	9.87	9.99	10.12	10.25	10.37	10.50	10.63	10.76	10.89	11.02	11.15	11.29	11.42	11.56	11.69	11.83	11.97	12.10	12.24	12.38
10	11	131	9.93	10.05	10.18	10.30	10.43	10.56	10.68	10.81	10.94	11.08	11.21	11.34	11.47	11.61	11.75	11.88	12.02	12.16	12.30	12.44
10	10	130	9.98	10.11	10.23	10.36	10.48	10.61	10.74	10.87	11.00	11.13	11.26	11.40	11.53	11.66	11.80	11.94	12.07	12.21	12.35	12.49
10	9	129	10.04	10.17	10.29	10.42	10.54	10.67	10.80	10.93	11.06	11.19	11.32	11.45	11.59	11.72	11.86	11.99	12.13	12.27	12.41	12.55
10	8	128	10.10	10.22	10.35	10.47	10.60	10.73	10.86	10.99	11.12	11.25	11.38	11.51	11.64	11.78	11.91	12.05	12.19	12.32	12.46	12.60
10	7	127	10.16	10.28	10.41	10.53	10.66	10.79	10.92	11.04	11.17	11.31	11.44	11.57	11.70	11.84	11.97	12.11	12.24	12.38	12.52	12.66
10	6	126	10.22	10.35	10.47	10.60	10.72	10.85	10.98	11.10	11.23	11.36	11.50	11.63	11.76	11.89	12.03	12.16	12.30	12.44	12.58	12.71
10	5	125	10.28	10.41	10.53	10.66	10.78	10.91	11.04	11.17	11.30	11.43	11.56	11.69	11.82	11.95	12.09	12.22	12.36	12.50	12.63	12.77
10	4	124	10.35	10.47	10.60	10.72	10.85	10.97	11.10	11.23	11.36	11.49	11.62	11.75	11.88	12.02	12.15	12.28	12.42	12.56	12.69	12.83
10	3	123	10.41	10.54	10.66	10.78	10.91	11.04	11.16	11.29	11.42	11.55	11.68	11.81	11.94	12.08	12.21	12.35	12.48	12.62	12.76	12.89
10	2	122	10.48	10.60	10.72	10.85	10.97	11.10	11.23	11.36	11.48	11.61	11.74	11.88	12.01	12.14	12.27	12.41	12.54	12.68	12.82	12.96
10	1	121	10.54	10.67	10.79	10.91	11.04	11.17	11.29	11.42	11.55	11.68	11.81	11.94	12.07	12.20	12.34	12.47	12.61	12.74	12.88	13.02
10	0	120	10.61	10.73	10.86	10.98	11.11	11.23	11.36	11.49	11.62	11.75	11.88	12.01	12.14	12.27	12.40	12.54	12.67	12.81	12.94	13.08

Appendix IV

SOURCES OF INFORMATION

It is the business of a realtor to know about conditions prevalent in the area in which he or she operates. Very frequently, realtors prepare information packets describing local demographics, the school situation, and the tax structure. These packets are available for the asking. Local realtors can be located through the National Association of Realtors or in the yellow pages.

The organizations listed herein furnish various kinds of information relating to real estate. Some are privately run and others are funded from state or federal sources. Because the real-estate market in every state operates in its own peculiar way, it is difficult to specify where one can get help. However, if you have a question, chances are that contacting one or more of these organizations will give you a satisfactory answer.

REAL-ESTATE ORGANIZATIONS

AMERICAN COLLEGE OF REAL ESTATE CONSULTANTS

2976 Highland Blvd.
Mound, MN 55364
Phone: (612) 472-2245
Founded: 1972. Members: 333. Staff: 5. Individuals proficient in the fields related to the real-estate profession (sales, accounting, law, consultation, education, finance, and government). Confers designation of Certified Real Estate Consultant (CREC), which is "symbolic of the highest professional attainment in the real-estate profession." Maintains library. Compiles statistics. Maintains placement and referral services. Publications: (1) Journal, irregular; (2) Digest, irregular; (3) Directory, annual.

AMERICAN SOCIETY OF REAL ESTATE COUNSELORS

430 N. Michigan Ave.
Chicago, IL 60611
Phone: (312) 440-8091
Founded: 1953. Members: 450. Staff: 4. Professional society of realtors with extensive experience in all phases of real estate, who provide a counseling service for which they receive compensation on a fee, per diem, or retainer basis, as opposed to a commission basis. Publications: (1) *The Counselor,* quarterly; (2) *Real Estate Issues,* semiannual; (3) Directory, annual. Affiliated with: National Association of Realtors.

NATIONAL ASSOCIATION OF REAL ESTATE APPRAISERS

853 Broadway
New York, NY 10003
Phone: (212) 673-2300
Founded: 1965. Members: 1000. Staff: 4. Qualified real-estate appraisers. "To make available the services of the most highly qualified real-estate appraisers." Publications: *National Roster,* annual.

NATIONAL ASSOCIATION OF REAL ESTATE BROKERS

1025 Vermont Ave., N.W., Suite 1111
Washington, DC 20005
Phone: (202) 638-1280
Founded: 1947. Members: 5000. Members of the real-estate industry. Research and educational programs include: Real Estate Management Brokers Institute; National Society of Appraisers; United Mortgage Bankers of America. Conducts educational seminars. Publications: (1) *Realtist Flyer,* weekly; (2) *NAREB Report,* monthly; (3) *Realtist Magazine,* annual.

NATIONAL ASSOCIATION OF REALTORS

430 N. Michigan Ave.
Chicago, IL 60611
Phone: (312) 440-8000
Founded: 1908. Members: 492,855. Staff: 375. Federation of 50 state and 1698 local real-estate board associations whose members are called Realtors (164,593) and Realtor-Associates (328,262), terms registered by the association in the U.S. Patent Office and in the States. Promotes education, high professional standards, and modern techniques in specialized real-estate work such as broker-

age, appraisal, property management, land development, industrial real estate, farm brokerage, and counseling. Conducts research programs. Sponsors a program of realtor involvement in service projects in their communities. Maintains extensive library and reference service. Departments: Convention and Exhibit, Economics and Research; Education; Government Affairs; Member Services; Public Relations. Publications: (1) *Realtors Review,* monthly; (2) *Real Estate Today,* 10/year; (3) *Journal of Property Management,* bimonthly; (4) *Appraisal Journal,* quarterly; (5) *National Roster of Realtors,* annual; also publishes and produces numerous booklets, lecture outlines, and promotional materials. Affiliated with: American Chapter, International Real Estate Federation; American Institute of Real Estate Appraisers; American Society of Real Estate Counselors; Farm and Land Institute; Institute of Real Estate Management; Real Estate Securities and Syndication Institute; Realtors National Marketing Institute; Society of Industrial Realtors; Women's Council of Realtors.

SOCIETY OF REAL ESTATE APPRAISERS (SREA)
Seven S. Dearborn St.
Chicago, IL 60603
Phone: (312) 346-7422
Founded: 1935. Members: 19,000. Staff: 46. Local Groups: 188. Professional society of full-time professional appraisers, analysts, and others having general need for appraiser information but primarily employed by real-estate and building businesses, savings and loan associations, life insurance companies, commercial and mutual savings banks, mortgage banking firms, and government agencies. Special chapter committees prepare cost reports, land value surveys, market data, and market trend reports. Committees: Chapter Services; Editorial; Educational; Public Affairs; Public Relations; SRA Admissions; SREA Admissions. Publications: (1) *Appraisal Briefs,* weekly; (2) *Appraisal Tapes,* bimonthly; (3) *The Real Estate Appraiser,* bimonthly; (4) Directory, annual; also publishes numerous books and pamphlets, including a *Guide Series on Appraising Apartments, Appraising Industrial Property, Appraising Residences,* and *Feasibility Analysis.*

MISCELLANEOUS

AMERICAN BAR ASSOCIATION (Legal) (ABA)
1155 E. 60th St.
Chicago, IL 60637

Phone: (312) 947-4000
Founded: 1878. Members: 220,000. Staff: 521. Affiliated Groups: 22. Attorneys in good standing at the bar of any state. Sponsors Law Day USA; maintains library and numerous committees. Maintains office in Washington, DC.

U.S. BUREAU OF THE CENSUS

The census bureau is a general-purpose statistical agency which collects, tabulates, and publishes a wide variety of statistical data about the people and the economy of the nation. These data are utilized by the Congress, by the executive branch, and by the public.

For further information, contact the Public Information Office, Bureau of the Census, Department of Commerce, Washington, D.C. 20233. Phone: (301) 763-7273.

U.S. DEPARTMENT OF HOUSING AND URBAN DEVELOPMENT (HUD)

HUD administers programs involving the financing, production, conservation, and rehabilitation of the housing stock. Mortgages and loans may be insured by HUD to aid in the purchase of single-family houses. Following is a list of all HUD field offices.

Region	Address/Phone
I. BOSTON, MASS. 02203	John F. Kennedy Federal Bldg. 617-223-4066.
Area Offices:	15 New Chardon St., 617-223-4111.
Boston, Mass. 02114	
Massachusetts, Rhode Island.	
Hartford, Conn. 06103	1 Financial Plaza, 203-244-3638.
Connecticut.	
Manchester, N.H. 03101	Norris Cotton Federal Bldg., 275 Chestnut St.,
Maine, New Hampshire, Vermont.	603-669-7011.
Insuring Offices:	
Bangor, Maine 04401	Federal Bldg. and Post Office, 207-942-8271.
Providence, R.I. 02903	Post Office Annex, 401-528-4351.
Burlington, Vt. 05401	Federal Bldg., 802-832-6274.
II. NEW YORK, N.Y. 10007	26 Federal Plaza, 212-264-8068.
Area Offices:	
Camden, N.J. 08103	519 Federal St., 609-757-5081.
Southern New Jersey.	
Newark, N.J. 07102	Gateway 1 Bldg., Raymond Plaza, 201-645-3010.
Northern New Jersey.	
Buffalo, N.Y. 14202	560 Main St., 716-842-3510.
New York, N.Y. 10019	666 5th Ave., 212-399-5290.
Eastern New York State.	
Caribbean Area Office, 00917	Federal Office Bldg., Carlos Chardon Ave.,
Puerto Rico, Virgin Islands.	Hato Rey, P.R., 809-763-6363.

Region	Address/Phone
II. NEW YORK—Continued	
Insuring Office:	
Albany, N.Y. 12207	Leo W. O'Brien Federal Bldg., Clinton Ave. & N. Pearl St., 518-472-3567.
III. PHILADELPHIA, PA. 19106	6th and Walnut Sts., 215-597-2560
Area Offices:	
Washington, D.C. 20009	1875 Connecticut Ave. N.W., 202-673-5837.
Washington Metropolitan Area.	2 Hopkins Plaza, 301-962-2121.
Baltimore, Md. 21201	625 Walnut St., 215-597-2645.
Maryland.	
Philadelphia, Pa. 19106	Two Allegheny Center, 412-644-2802.
Eastern Pennsylvania, Delaware.	
Pittsburgh, Pa. 15212	701 E. Franklin St., 804-782-2721
Western Pennsylvania, West Virginia.	
Richmond, Va. 23219	919 Market St., 302-571-6330.
Virginia.	
Insuring Offices:	
Wilmington, Del. 19801	New Federal Bldg., 304-343-6181.
Charleston, W. Va. 25301	1371 Peachtree St. N.E., 404-881-5585.
IV. ATLANTA, GA. 30309	
Area Offices:	
Birmingham, Ala. 35233	15 S. 20th St., 205-254-1617.
Alabama.	
Jacksonville, Fla. 32204	661 Riverside Ave., 904-791-2626.
Florida.	
Atlanta, Ga. 30303	230 Peachtree St. N.W., 404-221-4576.
Georgia.	
Louisville, Ky. 40201	601 S. Floyd St., 502-582-5251.
Kentucky.	
Jackson, Miss. 39213	300 Woodrow Wilson Blvd. W., 601-969-4703.
Mississippi.	
Greensboro, N.C. 27408	415 N. Edgewood St., 919-378-5363.
North Carolina.	
Columbia, S.C. 29201	1801 Main St., 803-755-5591.
South Carolina.	
Knoxville, Tenn. 37919	1111 Northshore Dr., 615-637-9300.
Tennessee.	
IV. ATLANTA, GA.—Continued	
Insuring Offices:	
Coral Gables, Fla. 33134	3001 Ponce de Leon Blvd., 305-445-2561.
Tampa, Fla. 35679	4224-28 Henderson Blvd., P.O. Box 18165, 813-228-2501.
Memphis, Tenn. 38103	100 N. Main St., 901-534-3141.
Nashville, Tenn. 37203	801 Broadway, U.S. Courthouse, Federal Bldg. Annex, 615-749-5521.
V. CHICAGO, ILL. 60606	300 S. Wacker Dr., 312-353-5680.
Area Offices:	
Chicago, Ill. 60602	1 N. Dearborn St., 312-353-7660.
Illinois.	
Indianapolis, Ind. 46205	4720 Kingsway Dr., 317-269-6303.
Indiana.	

Region	Address/Phone

V. CHICAGO—Continued

Detroit, Mich. 48226
Michigan.
 Patrick V. McNamara Bldg., 477 Michigan Ave., 313-226-7900.

Minneapolis-St. Paul, Minn. 55435
Minnesota.
 6400 France Ave., S. Minneapolis, 612-725-4704.

Columbus, Ohio 43215
Ohio.
 60 E. Main St., 614-469-7345.

Milwaukee, Wis. 53203
Wisconsin.
 744 N. 4th St., 414-224-1493.

Insuring Offices:

Springfield, Ill. 62704 — 524 S. 2d St., P.O. Box 1628, 217-525-4414.

Grand Rapids, Mich. 49505 — 2922 Fuller Ave. N.E., 616-456-2225.

Cincinnati, Ohio 45202 — Federal Office Bldg., 513-684-2884.

Cleveland, Ohio 44144 — 777 Rockwell Ave., 216-522-4065.

VI. DALLAS, TEX. 75202 — Federal Office Bldg., 214-749-7401.

Area Offices:

Little Rock, Ark. 72201
Arkansas.
 1 Union National Plaza, 501-378-5401.

New Orleans, La. 70113
Louisiana.
 1001 Howard Ave., 504-589-2063.

Oklahoma City, Okla. 73102
Oklahoma.
 301 N. Hudson St., 405-231-4891.

Dallas, Tex. 75201
New Mexico; eastern, northern, and western Texas.
 2001 Bryan Tower, 214-749-1601.

San Antonio, Tex. 78285
Southwest Texas.
 410 S. Main Ave., P.O. Box 9163, 512-229-6800.

Insuring Offices:

Shreveport, La. 71120 — 500 Fannin St., 318-226-5385.

Albuquerque, N. Mex. 87110 — 625 Truman St. N.E., 505-766-3251.

Tulsa, Okla. 74152 — 1708 Utica Sq., P.O. Box 4054, 918-581-7435.

Fort Worth, Tex. 76102 — Federal Bldg., 817-334-3233.

Houston, Tex. 77046 — 2 Greenway Plaza East, 713-226-4335.

Lubbock, Tex. 79408 — Courthouse and Federal Office Bldg., 806-762-7265.

VII. KANSAS CITY, MO. 64106 — Federal Office Bldg., 816-374-2661.

Area Offices:

Kansas City, Kans. 66101
Kansas, Western Missouri.
 4th and State Sts., 816-374-4355.

Omaha, Nebr. 68106
Iowa, Nebraska.
 7100 W. Center Rd., 402-221-9301.

St. Louis, Mo. 63101
Eastern Missouri.
 210 N. 12th St., 314-425-4761.

Insuring Offices:

Des Moines, Iowa 50309 — Federal Bldg., 515-284-4512.

Topeka, Kans. 66603 — 700 Kansas Ave., 913-234-8661.

VIII. DENVER, COLO. 80202 — Executive Tower, 1405 Curtis St., 303-837-4513.

Insuring Offices:

Denver, Colo. 80202 — 909 17th St., 303-837-2441.

Helena, Mont. 59601 — 610 Helena Ave., 406-449-5237.

Fargo, N. Dak. 58102 — Federal Bldg., P.O. Box 2483, 701-237-5771.

Region	Address/Phone

VIII. DENVER—Continued

Sioux Falls, S. Dak. 57102 — Federal Bldg. and U.S. Courthouse, 605-336-2980.

Salt Lake City, Utah 84147 — 125 S. State St., 801-524-5237.

Casper, Wyo. 82601 — Federal Office Bldg., P.O. Box 580, 307-265-5550.

IX. SAN FRANCISCO, CALIF. 94102 — 450 Golden Gate Ave., P.O. Box 36003, 415-556-4752.

Area Offices:

Los Angeles, Calif. 90057 — 2500 Wilshire Blvd. 213-688-5973.
Arizona, southern California.

San Francisco, Calif. 94111 — 1 Embarcadero Center, 415-556-2238.
Northern California, Hawaii, Nevada, Guam, American Samoa.

Honolulu, Hawaii 96813 — 1000 Bishop St., P.O. Box 3377, 808-546-2136.

Insuring Offices:

Phoeniz, Ariz. 85002 — 244 W. Osborn Rd., P.O. Box 13468, 602-261-4435.

Fresno, Calif. 93721 — Federal Bldg., 1130 O St., 209-487-5036.
Sacramento, Calif. 95809 — 801 I St., P.O. Box 1978, 916-440-3471.
San Diego, Calif. 92112 — 880 Front St., P.O. Box 2648, 714-293-5310.
Santa Ana, Calif. 92701 — 34 Civic Center Plaza, 714-836-2451.
Reno, Nev. 89505 — 1050 Bible Way, P.O. Box 4700, 702-784-5356.

X. SEATTLE, WASH. 98101 — 1321 2d Ave., 206-442-5415.

Area Offices:

Portland, Oreg. 97204 — 520 SW 6th Ave., 503-221-2561.
Southern Idaho, Oregon, Washington (counties of Clark, Klickitat, and Skamania).

Seattle, Wash. 98101 — 1321 2d Ave., 206-442-7456.
Alaska, northern Idaho, Washington (except Clark, Klickitat, and Skamania Counties).

Insuring Offices:

Anchorage, Alaska 99501 — 334 W. 5th Ave., 907-265-4790.
Boise, Idaho 83705 — 419 N. Curtis Rd., 208-342-2232.
Spokane, Wash. 99201 — W. 920 Riverside Ave., 509-456-4571.

INDEX